Changed Lives

Extraordinary Stories of Ordinary People

Peter R. Holmes
and
Susan B. Williams

Authentic

First published 2005 by Authentic Media
9 Holdom Avenue, Bletchley, Milton Keynes, Bucks,
MK1 1QR, UK
and 129 Mobilization Drive, Waynesboro, GA 30830-4575, USA
www.authenticmedia.co.uk

British Library Cataloguing in Publication Data
A catalogue record for this book is available from the
British Library

ISBN 1-86024-520-X

Photographs by Ian Giles www.iangilesphotos.co.uk
Cover design by Phil Houghton
Typesetting by Textype, Cambridge
Print Management by Adare Carwin
Printed by Haynes, Sparkford, Yeovil, Somerset, UK

Dedication

We dedicate this book to
Derry, Kate, John, Rebecca, Norma, Nicola,
Mike, Christine, James and Christa, Roman, Fiona,
Steve, Martin, Liam and Yvonne, all of whom have
been bold enough to tell their stories.

And to all at Christ Church Deal and the *Rapha*
fellowship, wherever they are meeting Jesus and
becoming who they were created to be.

Endorsements

'The idea that a faith community can both enable people in their spiritual journey and their therapeutic journey towards wholeness is enormously appealing and has been tantalisingly elusive – until now. The stories in this book point to the reality of a discipleship that heals. My hope is that the wider church hears these voices and starts out in this direction.'

Revd Alistair Ross, Head of Counsellor Training,
The Centre for Lifelong Learning, University of Birmingham

'Self-understanding is a precious gift only discovered in community. My visit to Christ Church was not what I expected; far from being centred on self-preservation, here is an enquiring public community focused on mutual service, which wants to know what it means to know the presence of God. Moreover, there is intellectual curiosity here – even puzzlement – not simply "counselling" as it is all too often understood.'

Revd Dr Kenneth Wilson OBE
Former Principal of Westminster College Oxford and Head of
Research, Queens Foundation, University of Birmingham

'We have been involved in the growth of CCD and the *Rapha* ministry since their inception, and our lives have been changed as a result. *Changed Lives* will give you an idea of the widely applicable principles of this work of the Lord. It is worth giving careful consideration to what the book is saying.'

Revd Francis and Marigold Pym

'The church in the West has lost its way. The Early Church was a place for sick people to find wholeness. Somehow, we started looking for well people, "sharp" people, "assets". The heart of Christ Church, Deal and Rapha returns the Gospel to the sick, because it believes that that is where Christ's heart is and it believes in the power of the Gospel.'

Revd Derry Long (USA)

'I've experienced first hand the amazing turnaround in people's lives as a result of being involved in filming a faith-based community. *Changed Lives* proves that there is something quite remarkable going on in a small corner of England, and more people should know about it.'

Paddy Wivell
Producer of the BBC2 TV documentaries
Love Will Tear Us Apart and *The Trouble with Jonny*, documenting
the lives of three people connected with Christ Church Deal.

Contents

Acknowledgements

A special thank you to Kate Riseley, Derry Long, Rebecca Mitchell, John Flicker, Nicola Carnall, Norma Davidson, Martin Carnall, Liam McCann, Roman von der Goltz, Fiona Burman, Steve Mitchell, James and Christa Allen, Yvonne Harrison, Christine Marsh and Mike Gregory for sharing their own stories in this book.

All initial editorial work, together with the collecting of a number of the stories was undertaken by Annie Frazer-Simpson, to whom we are indebted. Thank you Annie!

Thanks also to Ian Giles for his photographic work.

Introduction

Introducing the Book

This is a book of stories: stories of ordinary people, now living more extraordinary lives. Some had very 'average' day-to-day lives, and are now achieving something remarkable. Some were sick, and are now well. Some had broken relationships that are now restored. Some were living as Christians in disappointment and failure, but are now moving into relationship with Christ and into their futures with significant hope. But they all have one thing in common. They believe that the keys they found for their own growing wholeness, and the type of community they are part of, will also unlock healing, wholeness and greater Christlikeness for anyone who wants it.

Our message is simple: none of us needs to remain the way we are. Positive change is possible for everyone who wants it, for it is relationships that have made us sick, and so relationships must now help make us whole.

In essence, this book introduces some of the basic steps toward personal change that helps you become more like Jesus. We call this concept *therapeutic discipleship*. It is the idea that as we grow in our knowledge and experience of Jesus Christ we should also experience growth in wholeness. This wholeness in turn leads us to a greater depth of intimacy in knowing God, a greater capacity to meet Jesus. It is cyclic and integrated, whether you start with serious problems in your life or want to know Christ more intimately. Either way, each will build on the other if you wish it to.

To put it another way, this discipleship journey that heals is a way of approaching human need that on the one hand acknowledges we are all sick to varying degrees with a disease called sin, while on the other focusing on a Redeemer who is able to lead all of us out of our sicknesses. It is our hope that some of the experiences of the storytellers, and what they have learnt, may resonate with you in order to help you on your own personal journey towards both wholeness and a deepening life in Christ.

Introducing the 'Extraordinary People'

All these stories are written in the person's own words, either as they told their story to Annie, our editor, or as they wrote it down themselves. We have changed very little, so we hope you can feel you've met them. Those who 'talked' their story will still read as if they were speaking.

For your benefit these stories are grouped into key themes, such as loss, new careers, hearing God's voice, etc. Most themes are illustrated by two stories. To help you into each theme we have provided a brief intro- duction with a few general comments. Then at the end of each story we have drawn out and explained several principles on a practical level.

Some may accuse us of oversimplification or misrepre- sentation, because these stories are just a part of each person's life journey. But doing it this way allows us to focus on just one issue or area. In fact, all of us are actually very complex individuals, with many layers to our histories. So we don't want to give the impression that the one aspect of each person's life examined here is all they have done! Instead, this is a way of helping you, or those you are seeking to help, to focus and to have hope of being able to undo one specific area of damage.

This book, therefore, introduces in a somewhat novel way our journey both of becoming more whole and of meeting Jesus. These stories are not gleaned from just anyone anywhere who has a good story to tell, but from within a specific group of people living within a culture designed to lead each one into wholeness while they meet Jesus. So all the stories of people in this book are either members of our church, Christ Church in Deal, Kent, UK (CCD), or those who have benefited from our *Rapha* workshops (or Lifestream workshops, as they are sometimes known in the USA). We introduce ourselves, Christ Church and *Rapha* a little later, so that you have all the relevant background to understand where the stories are coming from. But first . . .

How Do You Best Use this Book?

We want to give you hope. We are going to assume that whoever you are, more hope would be a good thing! Perhaps you need hope because you'd like to see local churches offering a more consistent and effective way of helping people with deep-seated trauma and need. Perhaps one or more of the themes in this book are relevant to your own personal experience, or to someone you love, and you'd like to know how to tackle them. Or perhaps you have a pastoral responsibility and want to be able to offer support and wisdom to someone in need.

For clarity, we're going to assume that it's you who want to change and find something new, but we understand this may not be the case. If you are reading this to help others, the same principles apply.

We want to do much more than just tell you some interesting stories about our friends. (Yes, they are all personal friends of ours!) We want to take you on a journey with us, weaving through the personal adventures of the storytellers, but leaving you with more than memories. We want you to find hope of your own, for greater wholeness for yourself and others, and a new way, if you so wish, to meet Jesus. Christ is our Healer, our Redeemer and our Deliverer, from the despair and damage of our toxic pasts.

We want to tell you that whatever your condition or circumstances, Christ is able to meet you and help you, and we would like the privilege of helping to teach you how. Whether it is curiosity, despair, panic or even a psychotic breakdown, our hope is that you will find some hope in the following pages.

Yet we want you to find more than just the evidence of wholeness in this book. We do not want you to say after reading it, 'It's for them; they have a church and friends to help them. What about me?' We want you to know how you can start, and what you need to do next.

One of the key strengths of Christ Church Deal and the *Rapha* workshops is our desire to teach people the 'how to'. We so often hear the comment, 'OK, I know I've got a problem; now just tell me what to do.' In keeping with our practical-application approach, this book incorporates a whole range of principles that we draw out of the stories. These principles will help to teach you what to do, so you can apply them to your own life. Some of these ideas may shock you, others may confirm your worst fears, while others may witness with you as very true for you. It is the areas that most resonate with you that we want to help build with you.

For instance, you may have an addiction that you are not admitting to (alcohol, credit cards or sexual deviance?), or a problem with the male side of God's character.[1] The three addiction stories will help you to understand your place in this, and reading the stories will give you a range of practical things you can begin to do to help first own, and then break, the cycle of these disorders in your life. We are not unrealistic, however. It may need more than just this book to help you, so we have a range of extra resources that can offer you support if you want it, after reading the book – but more of that later.

Also, the way we have formatted this book gives it another practical application. It could be used as a home group study guide or Bible study aid. For instance, you can take one of the themes each week, read it ahead of time, and then discuss it when you meet. You will notice that we have deliberately not ended every sentence with large numbers of Bible verses, but as you read the stories you will note many of the principles have numerous Biblical ideas and practices behind them. Exploring Scripture will help you find them.[2]

Introducing Ourselves

We, Peter Holmes and Susan Williams, have had the privilege of being invited to bring these stories together in a book, as well as providing the background comments. We are on the Leadership Team of Christ Church Deal, UK, and we are also the ones who have written the material that is used in the *Rapha* workshops.

Peter's background has variety. He's a Londoner,

graduating from London Bible College in the early 1970s
and serving with Operation Mobilisation on the mission
field for several years in the Middle East, Asia and
Eastern Europe. He married Mary, from Sioux City, Iowa,
USA, and they lived for a time in the USA before
returning to England, where he worked for several
charities before going into business. He has also been
involved in planting several churches. But throughout
his life he has maintained an interest in helping people
find personal wholeness through a deepening
relationship with Christ. Over many years, allowing both
the Lord and those seeking help to teach him, he
developed an approach to wholeness in Christ that he
began to call healing discipleship. What he learnt he
shared, and his experience led him into a significant one-
to-one lay pastoral counselling ministry. He holds a
doctorate from the University of Birmingham, UK, in
therapeutic personal change, and social and group
processes in a faith setting.

Susan first came to Peter as a client in 1988. She was
very sick, suicidal, and tumbling into a second nervous
breakdown. She was close to being admitted to a
psychiatric hospital. Peter's approach to wholeness and
discipleship was like nothing she had ever experienced
before, and she eagerly set about learning all she could.
As her healing progressed she began teaching others
what she herself was learning, whilst also continuing her
career as a management consultant. Her own story,
which introduces many of the principles in this book, is
published in *Letting God Heal*.[3] Susan is continuing her
own doctoral work at the University of Bristol,
researching these principles of positive personal change.

We have known each other for more than fifteen years,
and have been working together in business and
therapeutic work for more than ten years.

Before you start reading the stories, you may also find it very helpful to know a little more about Christ Church Deal, and also about our *Rapha* workshops. We believe this will help the stories 'live' for you. But if you would prefer to skip the next sections on Christ Church Deal and *Rapha*, do feel free.

What is Christ Church Deal?

Christ Church Deal (CCD) is an independent evangelical church with a difference. It calls itself an open therapeutic faith community. Membership currently runs at around 150, plus kids, and continues to grow. Many of its members are in the 20–45 age range, which has led it to adopt a specific set of postmodern values and practice. This type of culture is known sociologically as Gen X.[4]

The church was started in 1998 by five of us who wanted to create a safe place for people who were hurting, churched and unchurched alike. Because of our background in lay pastoral counselling and Susan's journey into wholeness, it was only natural that the congregation would focus on helping people who had lost their way or come from an emotionally or mentally ill background. When we founded the community a number joined straightaway, because we were already helping them.

Although everyone lives in their own home, as in most churches, the community has adopted from its birth a cluster of principles called 'therapeutic social rules'. These guidelines are normally more characteristic of a therapeutic journey of personal positive change than of a church. These 'rules' include such principles as 'admit it', 'it will hurt like hell but it's worth it', 'don't pretend', 'they already know', 'it's all right to cry' and 'it gets worse before it gets better'.

When someone joins CCD they are introduced to these unwritten social rules through the cut and thrust of relationships. This means that a precondition of wanting to be part of CCD or the *Rapha* movement it has birthed is that a person must be willing to admit they need to change in at least some areas of their lives. Personal complacency would be an obstacle.

So CCD could be described as a community culture of personal positive change, a place where personal change is expected and normal. This makes its culture different from that of many traditional churches, where personal or group therapeutic change is not normally a priority. A therapeutic community model is sometimes used in psychiatry and in detox centres, and even prisons, to help people learn how to change. But, unlike a traditional medical model of therapeutic community, as members grow in their wholeness in CCD they do not normally leave, but remain to help the next generation of members with their disorders and damage. This is one of the advantages of having a church culture at the core of the community. It also means that CCD can be lay-led by those who have ever-increasing capacity because they are becoming more whole. Also, it allows us to have a larger leadership team that can carry the load, as a therapeutic community does, rather than employing full-time staff and being reliant on a minister or pastor.

We have a leadership team of around twenty, with everyone giving the time they can spare. Many, like us (Susan and Peter), work part-time in other employments in order to be available to the community for the rest of the time. When new people enter the community, they will seek out help from those who are gaining wholeness in the areas where they are in need. With such a large therapeutic community it is very easy to find numerous folk with similar problems and backgrounds to those of the people joining the community. We describe this growing pool of help as a therapeutic group IQ. All the stories in this book, one way or another, reflect the benefits of living in this kind of community.

Such a therapeutic culture, however, is not for everyone. Some traditional Christians, for instance, may find the whole way of life uncomfortable or difficult, because they are at ease with their Christianity the way it is. They feel they have no reason to change. But for those of us who have lost our way on our spiritual journey, or are going through emotional disorder, or have dropped out of society or the church, or are wanting to find and live in a greater measure of honesty about their condition, such a community as ours can be ideal. We have no exclusion policy. But we are aware that communities like CCD are not for everyone.

The Diversity of CCD

Despite having so many 'sick' people, the make-up of the community is not a bunch of eccentric amateurs. Among our membership are those trained in working with learning disabilities and challenging behaviour, clinical pharmacists, mental health service researchers and counsellors, and several others moving into further education towards earning a PhD. But the therapeutic aspects of the community are not the only area with professional depth. CCD also has specialists in starting businesses, managing change and finance management, as well as social workers, nurses trained in community and midwifery, day care co-ordinators, physiotherapists and those able to train in life skills. Many brought these skills with them when they joined the community, but others are launching into new careers. Everyone in the community has a key contribution to make. Moreover, these personal aspects are not the only gift the community has to offer: it is also an 'open home' culture.

An 'Open Home' Culture

As we have already noted, as people get well in CCD they find a growing capacity to help others, so our personal learnt experience of wholeness becomes available to others in the community. For instance, many return to formal education, marry or find a career. But all learn how to become givers. Our homes and healing journeys become significant resources to the whole community, and beyond. Everyone enters CCD as a taker, but as they heal they learn to become givers. Many churches fail, and their leadership burns out, simply because they attract too many takers and know too little wholeness.

For instance, as most individuals in CCD mature in their journey they also become 'mentors' to newer members. In supporting these newer members they help resolve problems that the more mature member has already dealt with. In essence, this process is replicable, becoming a 'loving God, loving people' movement. For as we become more whole we also have a growing capacity to love. The social and group processes in the community, as well as the social rules, all promote this.

Our Therapeutic Philosophy

It is the belief in CCD and *Rapha* that if you want to become the person God created you to be, and are aware you are not yet that person, the Lord will be very eager to help you. So what we are describing here is a church that is different, having adopted a therapeutic philosophy. It has a different approach to wholeness, healthcare and discipleship, offering either low-key or intensive therapeutic programmes. It is able to offer support to cover a wide range of damage, including being unable to find or know God or to maintain friendships, as well as confronting addictions, psychotic breakdown and the fear of returning to normal life, etc.

For instance, although medication may help in some cases, most people at some time will feel the need to reduce their medication, with medical support, and begin to engage and let go of the toxic range of emotions they are carrying. A therapeutic faith community such as ours is an ideal place to do this, because it offers an ongoing culture of support, not relying on the one-to-one psychiatric or counselling relationship alone, either within or outside the church.

Our philosophy of healing is that even if a person has been very sick for many years, if they actually want to, they will eventually be able to move to a place where they are independently supporting themselves through their own natural and learnt skills.

It is also a 'reductionist' culture, in the sense that it reduces people's disorders to manageable bite-sized pieces. With the help of the therapeutic community culture and its mentoring network, this process is able to assist people in becoming the person they were created to be, instead of the person they have become.

Although diagnostic counselling is available when and if needed, the whole journey is more relational, developmental and progressive, focusing on personal responsibility for the learning of positive personal change. A number of the stories in this book will illustrate this very clearly. A ground rule is that a person must be *living* the healing journey before they can teach and mentor others. This is a key qualification for being part of a therapeutic faith community. To be a giver and/or mentor, one must have recovered from a damaged past, be a lifetime learner and desire to mentor and teach others.

So what we are describing is a type of church that has therapeutic change at its core, with a therapeutic journey assumed, and where the social relational processes allow one to tell one's own story (a narrative culture) and learn from others.

Introducing *Rapha*

But before you pack your bags and come to Deal, I should add that CCD is not the only way one can do this therapeutic journey. At the time we started the church we had a waiting list, mainly of women, needing help and support. We held our first *Rapha* workshop here in Deal. This has grown, so that now more than a thousand people have attended workshops in the UK, and more than three hundred in the USA.

The workshops are usually held over a weekend, from Friday evening to Sunday afternoon. We have two basic workshops for men and two for women; they are gender exclusive and different for each group. The first weekend introduces the basic principles that will help a person begin a 'therapeutic journey' with Christ, while the second weekend gives them the basic tools and shortcuts they will need to learn to be successful in sorting out their problems.[5] We then have an additional range of workshops (e.g. Meeting Jesus, Womanhood, Living with Healing) and training tapes, to give extra background and ideas for promoting change. Many of those who have attended workshops meet together regularly in regional discipleship groups to share the experience of their therapeutic journey and give each other support.

In a sense the models in CCD and *Rapha* are slightly different, in that the one in Christ Church has community support, whereas the *Rapha* one is more a personal journey, or one undertaken within a support group. But both offer the same journey with the same potential fruit.

One additional feature is common to both types of journey: diversity. No two people have the same needs, so no two people do the same journey. The principle is that Christ meets the individual where they are, and although most people's journeys will have some common themes, each journey will begin to track a unique path with the Lord and those sharing the journey with them. The way we have developed this programme means it can fit anyone, regardless of culture, experience or need. In some ways this book illustrates this simple fact.

One Final Comment . . .

CCD and *Rapha* stand for a very specific type of discipleship journey. We believe that most people, both inside and outside the church, want to become more fully human, to live a life of significance. But it is also our belief that to become more fully human we must also seek to become more Christlike. To become more Christlike we have to become more whole, and to become more whole means we all need to go on a journey of therapeutic personal positive change. In this book you will find numerous people from both sides of the Atlantic who are seeking successfully to do this. Let us now look at some specific problems people face, and join them on their journey.

Notes

[1] Many women, and even some men, have a problem with the idea of God being presented as male, e.g. the man Christ, especially when a person's past includes abuse by men. This can leave a person with very negative attitudes towards men.

[2] At the *Rapha* workshops we give folk a range of 'Bible Notes' that go into much more detail regarding the Biblical background to our practices. We have also completed a series in our Sunday Bible Studies, exploring *Rapha* principles throughout Scripture. See the 'Afterword' at the end of the book for more details.

[3] Williams, S.B., Holmes, P.R., *Letting God Heal: From Emotional Illness to Wholeness* (Milton Keynes: Authentic, 2004).

[4] For an introduction to other Gen X churches, see Flory, R.W., Miller, D.E., *Gen X Religion* (New York: Routledge, 2000).

[5] Our workshops in the USA are structured slightly differently.

1

Hearing God's Voice

These first two stories introduce you to two people. Kate was a single mum when she joined the community. She came without any faith in God, and was in such desperate need that relationship with God was the last thing on her mind. Derry was quite different. He is pastor of a large evangelical church in Oregon, USA. He has had a long friendship with me (Peter), spanning over twenty-five years.

Our community is a mixture of those who have a long history of relationship with God, and those who have none. In CCD and *Rapha* we deliberately avoid an emphasis on becoming a Christian when people first join us, but instead focus on meeting each person at their point of need. This was Jesus' approach. He first focused on people's needs and met those needs without conditions, and then either let them go or sent them away. It was only when people came back to Him on their own initiative, wanting a relationship with Him, that He invited them to commit to and serve Him. Many did come back and follow Him in this way (1 Cor. 15:6). Some seem to have taken their healing, left Jesus, and never returned to follow Him.

Kate and Derry both had very different needs. Jesus desires to minister to each, individually. For instance, Derry began to realize that some of his Christian practices over many years, rather than helping his Christian walk, had in fact created barriers between him and the Lord. So he needed to begin dismantling these concepts, ideas and practices. For Kate, the whole idea that people wanted to love her was overwhelming. What she would learn is that such a capacity to love, in those who sought to help her, was itself the fruit of other people's desire to change, with Jesus and the *Rapha*/CCD community helping them.

Both stories focus on the simple need for all of us to hear the voice of God. After you have read the stories, we will explain to you why it is so important for individuals to hear God's voice for themselves.

No One Was Listening
Kate Riseley

I'm 30, I was married two years ago, and I have three girls: Hannah (9), Charlotte (1), and Grace (newborn). I've lived in Deal since the age of 9. I've been at Christ Church for four-and-a-half years, but had no previous church background. I enjoy reading, writing and walking, and I love the sea.

I began surviving before I was born: I know that now. And that was the drive that kept me going through twenty-five years of abuse, neglect, petty crime and destructive relationships.

Somebody asked me the other day if I had any good memories of my mum, and I didn't at all. All I can remember is being abused, mainly emotionally. Physically also, to an extent, although it really didn't matter in the grand scheme of things, compared, that is, to how I was treated and how, as a result, I ended up feeling about myself.

It has only become 'abuse' since I've begun to learn about it on my journey, because at the time it was just normal. What I do remember, though, is always being a very little girl. I was very little in stature and she always seemed very, very big.

She was very sick, and because of that I could do no right. She had huge compulsions about cleanliness and tidiness, for example. And being a little girl, I would sometimes drop things or make a mess. At such times she hated the sight of me and would make that quite clear.

I wasn't allowed to touch her. She couldn't stand me touching her. It would be, 'Get off me,' 'Get away from me,' 'You're dirty and horrible.' So I would not touch her. But then the next day it would be the other way and she would maybe want to be touched. She'd raise her hand, suggesting a cuddle, and of course I'd withdraw with the fear of being hit. Then I'd be accused of not loving her. So I couldn't win. I just couldn't.

If I went to playgroup it would be, 'Just don't embarrass me today, don't do anything that's going to embarrass me.' So I learnt to be very withdrawn, because I didn't know how to 'not embarrass' her.

It was, 'Don't touch that, you'll break it,' so I couldn't help in the house. I was never allowed to touch the toaster, the kettle, the vacuum cleaner. But then I was reprimanded for not involving myself in the house. She would say, 'Look at the nice tea I've given you,' and I would freeze. 'Oh well, if it's not good enough for you, don't have it,' and she'd scrape it away into the bin, so I wouldn't have any tea.

She would give me Christmas presents, but I didn't know how to react, so they'd be thrown away, put in a black sack and given to a charity shop. I was locked outside on Christmas Day once because I didn't know how to react when she said we were having lamb, not turkey. I didn't know if I was supposed to say, 'Oh, that's nice,' or what. I didn't know what I was supposed to do, and no one was listening.

I remember her decorating one day, when she fell off the ladder and miscarried. It was my fault, because I'd looked at her and made her fall off the ladder. Another day she tried to kill herself. She said, 'I'm taking these pills. This is what you've made me do, because I just can't bear to be around you any more. You make my life hell. If it wasn't for you I'd have a life.' She took the tablets, lay down, and went to sleep. But they didn't work. So when she woke up that was also my fault.

I didn't know how to be or how to look. I was so afraid of doing the wrong thing that I just stopped reacting altogether. I became totally unresponsive. No one noticed.

My dad was an alcoholic. He wasn't abusive to me physically. Instead, he was abusive by his absence. He didn't save me from Mum; he didn't rescue me. Instead he allowed the abuse, and indirectly made it a lot worse. I looked like him and I acted like him, because he, too, was very withdrawn. Because of the way he made her feel, I then got beaten and, I suppose, everything she couldn't do to him she tried to do to me.

But all the time there was this middle-class front. We lived in a very nice house. On the face of it we ate very well. I knew how to behave and I could mix in any circles. We would often go to big hotels in London. My dad was a book dealer and I could speak to auctioneers, high-up people in the trade. I could eat with any amount of cutlery that was put in front of me. And no one knew . . . no one ever knew. No one was listening.

Sometimes she would call in Social Services and I'd be accused of violence and aggression. Sometimes school would call them in because they'd seen marks, but she was very clever and I was never heard. If I was about to be heard, she would swoop in; she was very eloquent and very well presented. She certainly didn't look or act like a woman who would do this. She was never caught and it was always projected onto me.

She actually put me out there to be found. I've been seeing psychiatrists since I was diagnosed clinically depressed at the age of 5. There were mountains of records on me and all the time it was her. They say that she had 'Munchausen's Syndrome by Proxy'.

When I think back, I just lived my life in absolute terror and continued building up this store of immense anger and 'Why?'. Why was no one there for me? The people from Social Services would arrive and I'd think, 'Oh, thank God they're here,' but they would be saying, 'Why won't you just try to love your mother, Kate?' And she'd be looking at me: 'Don't you dare, don't you dare tell them.' And I'd stand there, knowing I was going to be beaten when they left, but being blamed for not reacting the way I should. They never knew. No one was listening.

When I was about 9 we moved to Deal and soon after that my parents separated. The abuse got a lot worse, a lot more overt. I was put into a children's home because I was so bad. I was in with children who had severe attachment disorders and severe behavioural problems. I was in with juvenile arsonists, burglars, abusers. I was abused in that home just by being taunted and bullied, and the boys would tie me up and leave me so that when the dinner bell went I would be punished for not coming down on time. I didn't know what was happening. I still thought the system would rescue me, but it never did. No one was listening.

Then one day after I was back with her, when I was 11, my mum just said, 'You stay here or you go to your dad.' So I went to school that day and never went home. I went to my dad's, but he was an alcoholic and never at home. I would go to his shop to get some money for food and there'd be a note on the door saying, 'Gone to the Post Office,' but he wouldn't come back for three or four days.

So I lived in a flat with no electricity, no gas, absolutely nothing, and I never got found. That's part of the damage – I never got found. I remember scrubbing my school shirts with a nailbrush and soap, trying to clean them. I'd made it to the girls' grammar school because I was academically bright, but of course I was bullied and teased because I was such a mess.

Dad just never came home. So I learnt to steal. I stole money to eat, but kept this middle-class outlook. I was at the girls' grammar, with my satchel, dictionary, Bible and fountain pen, but stealing and becoming a liar because I also couldn't be disloyal. I used to go to my friend Sarah's house and say I'd lost my key. I would do anything not to get Dad into trouble. Then he lost his shop but never told me. I just walked in when the bailiffs were taking every-thing.

Then I went out to work, and worked from that point on. I didn't have to be a schoolgirl any longer, pretending that Dad was there at home. I went to college and did community care training. I was smoking, drinking, doing drugs, latching on to anyone I could, desperately trying to find family. So in the house where the bed-sit was I tried to be part of the family, but couldn't really succeed because I wasn't very nice. I had a real attitude problem, and always fell in with the wrong crowd. I was on a path of self-destruction. No one noticed.

I was working hard but I was out drinking heavily every night, clubbing, going into work straight from the club. I'd get home at five in the morning and be at work at seven.

I was always trying to be grown up, always trying to be something I wasn't. But I was very capable. I've been quite high up in whatever I do, or frustrated that I couldn't be higher. I had nothing to prove that I could do that. I got by. I 'blagged' my way through, talked my way in, got through on attitude. But I was so alone. I was always in debt, never paid any bills, never paid any rent. As soon as I got caught I would move on.

I was just running, repeating the cycle my mum had lived. One day I'd go to the doctor and be crying out for

Changed Lives

help. I'd want psychiatric help, to be locked away, so I would manufacture illnesses. Then they'd knock on the door, but I'd hide in my bed.

By this time I'd become very manipulative. I knew a group of guys, and I convinced one of them to rent me a room in his house. I had every intention of making sure I had a relationship with him, but I said I'd be the lodger. So I was the lodger, but of course I wasn't, I was just a 'live-in'. We slept together, but had almost no relationship, yet we were kind of together in a funny sort of way. I lived with him for three years and that's where I had Hannah, my eldest daughter. I was 21.

For the next three or four years I continued that crazy lifestyle, doing everything to excess, not paying the bills, running, risking my daughter, but all the time being angry and wanting revenge, while at the same time wanting my dream family. I began having affairs with married men. That's how I came to fall pregnant again, by someone I wished I could have had the chance to love properly, but this time I miscarried.

At the hospital they told me I'd had a 'spontaneous abortion', whereas I felt my baby was dead. Six months later there was still no one listening. All that time, I'd been on the waiting list for counselling. At this point my doctor changed my medication because of my thoughts of self-harm. He also ensured my counselling began immediately.

However, although the counselling was very pro-fessional, and they were very kind, it actually pushed me nearer the edge. Firstly there was the way they approached my miscarriage. Like the hospital, they wouldn't let me talk about her, and I knew 'her' was right. My baby had been a girl. But they insisted it was merely a spontaneous abortion. They argued that at that early stage no one could have known. They told me I should move on, say goodbye to the incident. But I knew she was a person, she wasn't just an incident. No one was listening.

Secondly, every week in the counselling I was being 'undone'. Memories I had spent my life suppressing were being unlocked and brought to the surface, but then I was left to walk around with them all hanging out until the next appointment.

At that time I had no knowledge of a spiritual dimension, or Jesus, or anything like that, but I did have my 'little voice'. It was not audible, but more like an instinct, which always stuck up for me in a kind way that no one else ever had.[1] And the more I spoke like that, about the baby and the little voice, the more concerned my counsellor became. This in turn triggered my survival instincts. I feared they would 'section' me, that is put me away for my own safety, as they would see it. But I'd lose my daughter. So I stopped seeing the counsellor.

I always knew the little voice wasn't part of being ill. I proved that when I got to Christ Church. As I progressed in my healing journey, the little voice that wasn't heard and had learnt to excuse herself, be quiet, almost get drowned, but had somehow remained there, was now getting bigger, more excited and stronger. It was also getting more comfortable.

Before this, the little voice had been merely an extra, an alien, a foreign body saying, 'Don't do this to yourself.' It was rootless, like something floating around the system, all the time trying to be heard. And when I learnt to meet Jesus, it was only that little voice that He talked to, and she felt grounded. She wasn't just trying to be heard. It was natural and I didn't doubt. But that came later. Things would have to get a lot worse before they got better.

It was during that time, following the miscarriage, that I first heard about Christ Church. I was still in touch with my close friend from school, Sarah. I also knew her brother and watched him become emotionally very ill. When I had become really ill myself, after the miscarriage, he came to see me. He had so obviously changed and found a way of getting well. He told me about Christ Church and how Susan and Peter had helped him to find healing. But because it was a church, I wrote it off straightaway.

I judged them because it was Christian-based. I thought God was this theological booming voice that came out of Heaven and, being so bad, I knew I'd just get struck down by Him. But that wasn't the Jesus that I finally met. And had I not reached the end of the road, with God watching on, I would never have taken the time to find out what He was really like. Part of me would have judged Him and moved on, while the other part of me would have taken what she wanted and then moved on. Then I would have blamed everyone else for not listening.

Because of what I believed about myself, as a result of the early abuse, I had disqualified myself. I already knew I was bad. What had always been said must be true. I couldn't be helped, I wasn't allowed, because I was bad and should be punished. Even so, I did ring Susan, and after talking with me she sent me a tape. I never listened to it, putting it in a drawer with all my unopened bills.

Into yet another relationship, I found the life of my daughter, and my own, threatened as I came home one evening by the wife of a man I had been sleeping with and all of her neighbours. My maternal instinct kicked in – it was all I had left. I put my little girl behind me to shield her and managed to get to my front door. At that moment the husband returned, and helped us into the house, which of course infuriated the women even more. I called the police and they told me to put my daughter behind the sofa, as far away as possible from the front of the house. During the time it took me to do that, the wife had broken the door down and was in the house, fighting the man in the hall. Then the police arrived and we were taken out.

We stayed in a safe house for a few days. Although most of me remained numb, part of me was also panicking. I couldn't return, so where would I live? I actually saw him again in an attempt to secure a future. I almost did it, but then he went to visit his children. The wife had got the neighbours together and they all told him what they knew about me. He attempted suicide. I managed to stop him, but realized it was over. I contacted my friend Sarah, and she collected Hannah and me.

I spent a night at her parents' house, but they wanted me to see the doctor. Again alarm bells rang, so I ran. I was so determined to survive. Giving up was defeat, and I would die. I made Sarah drive me to her brother's house, remembering what he'd told me. He wasn't in and I was getting hysterical. I'd decided that if this didn't work, if I couldn't make contact with the people he'd told me about, I'd kill myself and leave Hannah to be cared for by Sarah. I couldn't face being sectioned or put in prison.

Then, and I don't know how or why, my little voice screamed at Sarah to take me to the house her brother had talked about, the house where Susan lives, Waterfront. Reluctantly Sarah took me. It was Mary, Peter's wife, who answered the door, and I collapsed into the hallway. Susan came and introduced herself – I don't remember anything that was said.

Practical help followed. There was no condemnation, no direct teaching about God. Hannah and I were just fed, bathed, housed and loved. Later I was supported through a round of meetings with police, the social services, everything that was necessary.

I'd finally stopped running, I'd handed myself in, I'd admitted defeat. And the very thing I thought would kill me now began to save my life. It was the thing I'd been holding on to that nearly killed me: 'I mustn't give up,' 'I will survive.' But when I finally let go and collapsed in a heap, then it became possible for others to help me back onto my feet.

It all felt like coming home. And since coming to Christ Church, becoming part of the community, I have found a family. I have been fathered, mothered, brothered and sistered, and now I'm married and have two more daughters. Everything I dreamed of and thought could never happen. And more.

Some time after I'd begun my journey, I was sitting one day with a member of Christ Church and I began to cry. They simply asked, 'What is it?' I replied without thinking, 'I miss my baby,' as simple as that. The person said, 'I'm sorry. Was it a boy or a girl?' I sobbed, 'It was a girl, called Rachel.' That was the first time my 'little voice' had ever been acknowledged without question. Someone was listening.

I simply sat looking at Rachel in my imagination, describing her to my friend.[2] It was hard to do, after all that time, and not being allowed to before. Then, when I was all talked out and all cried out, I gave her to this huge man called Jesus who took her to look after until I could meet her again, and I was content about the whole situation for the first time.

Peter and Susan were quite interested that I had given her to Jesus, considering they hadn't yet talked to me about Him. But I knew who He was now. He'd been there all the time, in the little voice. Someone had been listening.

Hearing the Voice of the Lord
Derry Long

I'm 55, American, and live in Portland, Oregon. I am married to Marlyce, and we have three grown-up kids. I've been a pastor and denominational leader for over thirty-five years in the Evangelical Church of North America. We host Rapha *Workshops – we call them* Lifestream *here in the USA. I've been doing the* Rapha *journey for several years. One of my favourite hobbies is reading.*

A crisis is an event or moment that requires more resources than I have. Sometimes they sneak up on us; sometimes they explode in our 'faith'. I met Peter Holmes when he and his family were living in Hinton, Iowa, USA. I dedicated their son Christopher when he was six months old. He is now 26. When I had my crisis I looked for something, or someone, to hold on to. I put out some feelers, including a letter to Peter, who had by then returned to England. A few months later the phone rang. 'Hello, mate. Let's meet in South Dakota.'

That was the beginning of my search to know and hear God. I thought I knew what it would look like. Not a clue. Some time later, when I was sitting in Peter's living room in Ramsgate, UK, he said, 'You are afraid of the supernatural.' I did not understand his statement. It did not register with anything in me, either intellectually or emotionally. I thought, 'Give me something I can use, something that fits.' As we finished, he invited me just to tell the Lord I was sorry for that fear.[3] I thought for a moment, then agreed. It was all a rather perfunctory exercise. I started to pray, saying sorry to the Lord, but evidently my spirit knew something my mind didn't, and I began to weep, wondering as I was doing so where these tears were coming from.[4] God was starting to talk. But His voice seemed so different to what I had expected. Then I realized that the voice I had usually heard and called God's was just my own.

Really, He had always been talking, but in a different voice. That was so hard to believe at the time. Peter is very abrupt. He is like a medic in an emergency room. Always aware of life and death, he seldom wastes time. His conversations have meaning. I was used to a God, had created a God, like a security blanket that was warm, fuzzy, safe. Oh, and I also used religious terms like faithful, loving etc. But instead I have had to learn that God is a warrior, looking for warriors. For me this was all an unexplored new world.

So I made a radical choice to let God offend me. He didn't have to be polite any more, work within my framework or leave me peaceful. It was the link to truth for me. Peter has often been God's battering ram in my life. The Lord would hear the invitation of my spirit, but I would be immobile. A bracing conversation from Peter, and God was talking. I don't have any trouble knowing the difference between Peter's voice and God's voice, but it is clear they are on the same side. If I am polite, it is almost always for my sake, to be accepted etc. Peter is willing not to be polite. It is one of the ways I know he cares about the journey of Christ in me. It was as if, when I told the Lord He could offend me, He knew I really wanted to hear Him. 'The offence of the Gospel' doesn't end, even for experienced believers in Christ.

I tell you it is dangerous, exciting, exhausting, but perhaps, more importantly for me, I know God is with me. This is something He promised in the Christmas story. Hearing His voice has caused me to change my job, change my friends, change my home, take risks, win, lose, and try again. His voice has caused me to align myself with His heart. His voice is intoxicating. I get angry at what he says, often. But I can't go back. It is one of the ways I know He loves me: He talks to me.

Not everyone is happy with me hearing God's voice. They feel He should talk to me their way. It has been a hard thing for me to accept that some people are more concerned with controlling the landscape of the Christian world than with celebrating people meeting the Lord. The more I hear His voice, the more I care about people. This in itself is a radical thing for me.

For many years I had known almost nothing of hearing God's voice. The window through which I had looked at reality was small. I saw little breadth. I spoke the words common to my tradition: 'having a personal relationship with Christ'. But there was little that was personal. I believed in Christ, believed I would go to heaven when I died, believed there were things He wanted me to do, and believed God gave us the Bible so I would know what He thought. This knowing relationship had been for me through reading a book considered 'personal'. Yet a personal relationship is all about talking, sharing, communicating in many ways, at many times, on many subjects. It is ongoing, and should be connected to daily life.

For instance, as I read the gospel of John, our Lord began to remind me that fruitfulness is related to intimacy and depends on His words remaining in me. Also, in John 10:4 Jesus says, 'His sheep ... know his voice.' Fifteen times in the New Testament we find the phrase, 'He who has ears to hear, let him hear.' Likewise, Jesus is called the Word in John 1, and says that just as food nourishes the body, so communication from Him nourishes the soul. In Revelation 3:20 the Lord says, 'If anyone hears my voice . . .'

Along similar lines the Apostle Paul suggests, 'Faith comes by hearing . . .', while in the Old Testament, 2 Chronicles 20:15-17 is just one of many examples in the Bible of God speaking: 'This is what the Lord says to you . . .'

What all this suggested to me was that God is a talker who reveals truth about Himself, the world, others, the spiritual world and even me. And He wants to be in relationship with me not as a Master with His servant or slave, but as friend with friend. He says that because I am His friend He wants to tell me everything He knows from His Father.

What I began to see is that He talks in a wide range of ways, through the Scriptures, through pictures and visions, through other people, through natural phenomena, through supernatural phenomena, through impressions, through words, through angels, through dreams. Wow! Why would I not feel loved? He met with Adam and Eve, told Abraham to move, sent an angel to wrestle with Jacob, gave Joseph a vision, spoke to Moses through a burning bush, used a pillar of fire and a cloud to give direction, thundered on Mount Sinai, ministered through an angel to Gideon and Daniel, gave Peter a vision of unclean animals made clean, walked as glorified Christ with the men on the Emmaus road, and gave visions to the Apostle John on the island of Patmos. I no longer wanted to consider these incidents as only historical settings for meaning, but as the experiential realities of an innovative, creative God who speaks in many languages, and numerous ways, to me.

But some things I struggled with as I moved towards this adventure in conversation with God. One was my need to face up to how tainted modern Christianity is with the residue of the eighteenth-century Enlightenment. For instance, its teaching that all reality is experienced and validated by human reason, which elevates my mind above all my other faculties, including my emotions and personal will. This has the effect of making anything I do which does not fit the understanding of my mind feel dangerous, thereby preventing the Lord from using my emotions through, say, the book of Psalms, which is filled with emotion. This in turn forces me to lower the ceiling on how much supernatural reality I can participate in within my personal paradigm. This mind barrier was daunting, so it took me a considerable time to overcome it. But I continued to sense the Lord's approval in my journey, because it was all about meeting Him.

A second struggle was my own fallenness, and hence my desire to stay in control. Part of this urge moves me to live exclusively in material reality. When Mary Magdalene met Jesus after His ascension, she grabbed hold of him, and Christ needed to say, 'Mary, you have to let me go.' She wanted to keep him in the material world. If I were asked to choose whether having Jesus sitting across from me at the breakfast table was better than speaking to an unseen force, I would be inclined to say the former would be better. But Jesus Himself said it was better for me if He went away. This enlargement of my world from material to invisible, to see this all as part of the same universe, was difficult. It required me to develop an eye for different things: the feelings in a room, the swiftly worded disclaimer, the change in posture, the picture or dream.

Thirdly, there was the fear of getting it wrong. I had to

learn that such fear was based not on my inability as a receiver but on my distrust of the sender. This I had to face. It is funny that at a human level, when I am in conversation with my friends, I do not fear getting it wrong.

This next one has been the most painful. I have had to deal with my fear of the hidden, and not so hidden, scorn of other believers. It is the mocking of those Christians who have a model of spirituality with which they are satisfied but also somehow feel compelled to require others to conform to it. The response, when I have refused to submit in this way, has been anger, rejection and even slander. All, I might add, under the righteous heading of protecting 'the Lord' and 'His truth'. But today, for me, the sound of His voice has a richness that overshadows the cry of others who might be ordering me to get in step. To hear the voice of the Lord is one of the most life-giving realities I can imagine.

I have now come to expect to hear the Lord. He talks to me about me, about others and about himself. Remember that disastrous choice by Adam and Eve which led to a breakdown of communion. They hid from themselves, from each other and from God. God's speaking involves redemption of these three areas. Here's how it has been working out in my life:

To me about me. Recently I have been in a spiritual battle. Someone gave me a picture that included three large pillows, and told me the Lord had said they were for me. I asked the Lord about it, and the word 'peace' came to me. A day later I was having coffee with Jonathan, a friend. I was ready to leave when he said that he didn't feel our conversation was over. Then he said, 'I asked the Lord about our meeting, and the word 'peace' came to me, and I knew I was supposed to give it to you. I don't know what it means.' It is such life to me to know that in the midst of my struggle God is telling me to rest, to experience His peace.

I realized that from childhood I had carried in my spirit a rejection of my physical appearance. A woman came to me and said the Lord had given her a word for me. The word was from an old song: 'You must have been a beautiful baby.' I said to her, 'You couldn't have known.'

To me about others. A lovely young woman came to see me. I asked the Lord what it was about, and I saw a volcano. We talked at length and all her questions had to do with child-rearing, so I concluded the picture was of no relevance. As she got up to leave, she turned and said, 'By the way, I have been struggling with violent outbursts of temper that I can't seem to conquer.' I shared the picture with her to assure her that the Lord was interested in that problem and had something to say to her on the matter.

I was with a woman, but I felt she was never present to me when I talked to her.[5] I had felt that before. I carelessly blurted out, 'You know, when I am with you, it is like you don't exist.' Tears welled up in her eyes, and she said, 'But I want to exist.' If you hate something you won't choose to spend a lot of time with it, and if you hate yourself you will find reasons not to be present to yourself. So began a journey for her of seeing herself as God sees her.

I was meeting an influential Christian leader, apparently at the top of his game. As I drove to the meeting I felt I should tell him that the Lord was pleased with him, and encourage him to stay on the course he was on. We had lunch, but I struggled to find a place that felt appropriate. Finally, as we were near to leaving, I just said it. Tears came to his eyes. He shared how other leaders had recently challenged him, and how much this affirmation from the Lord meant to him. It was significant because he knew I could not have known what he was going through, but the Lord knew.

To me about God. The Lord is showing to me that he is not the God I thought He was. He is far more whimsical, angry and unpredictable. He is far more than just my security blanket. Of the three areas He is speaking about, this is the newest to me as I write. The most significant reality He has communicated about Himself is that He is always present. One way He has done this is by telling others to tell me about the presence of His angels.

These stories are the tip of the iceberg of God's lively, purposeful discourse with me. Sometimes He just talks to me as one friend speaks to another. Sometimes He speaks requiring a response, and other times just to share. I have always understood that He loves me, but I never really thought He liked me. I accepted that He was obligated to love me, but to like is more a choice, and it didn't seem to me that if He was given a choice He would ever choose me. More than any other thing, His joy in talking to me has convinced me of His devotion and personal affection for me. This has been a great source of release. Communication is an act of love.

There is a voice regularly whispering into almost everyone's ear, suggesting we are disqualified from such lofty heights as hearing the Lord. Only the reassuring and recurring voice of the Lord beats away such a lie and reminds us that our Lord is delighted with our company.

Where to start? I started by asking questions. How does this look to you, Lord? What do I really want? Remember, the Lord asked that question of Bartimaeus, who was blind. You would think the answer would be obvious, but the Lord wanted him to speak it out. What do you have for this person, Lord?

I established boundaries, then submitted them to the

Lord. The Scriptures provided one. I never shared something with another person without them confirming in some way that I was meant to share it. God doesn't share something about someone so that I can judge him or her, but so that I can love him or her more wisely.

Am I ready to act? God shows up at the point of action.

I asked three young men what was the most important aspect of hearing the voice of the Lord. All three separately said, 'Being present to yourself.'[6] I remembered how Jesus told Peter the Apostle that he would deny his Lord. Peter was not present to himself, so wouldn't hear of it. When the Lord prayed for Peter, He did not pray that Peter would be strong and not deny Him, but that after he had done it, he would not become so discouraged as to give up. Jesus was helping Peter to become more present to himself. The Lord cannot deal with the idealized me, the pseudo me, the me in denial, but only with the real me. So I must require of myself that I be there, be present. To live fully in the real world is to know that I need His company.

I'm 54 as I write this. It did occur to me that I could have taken an optimistic view of my life – it had not really been that bad. There had been good moments, times of God's blessing. I had found a place to fit in, even advance. And if I were to move on, other people wouldn't understand. Why try to change things at this late date? I could have used that as an excuse to not go on this journey. But I didn't.

Some Comments

There is much in what Kate and Derry have said that we could elaborate on. But let us start by telling you why we put such emphasis on each person beginning to hear

God's voice for themselves. We all live in a world of hundreds of competing voices: advertising, our need to learn, television, friends and enemies, music and art, even computer games claim our hearing. The voices are endless. If we are unwell, for example, we hear lots of voices: doctors, therapists, well-meaning friends, pastors etc. All will probably have a valid contribution to make, but what we are suggesting in this book is that none of these should be the principal guiding voice in our lives.

Ultimately, what helps us best to centre, to become more whole, is learning how God sees us. This includes what He wants to say to us, how He wants to help us, and His telling us how we can best help ourselves. We are not saying you should ignore other voices, particularly medical advice, but suggesting that ultimately it is the voice of the Lord talking to us about ourselves that will probably prove most helpful. This will be particularly true if we can unpack what we are hearing with the support of those we trust. Many of us find ourselves in the place where we have tried every other option in order either to get to know God better or to get well, and the method and its many voices have not helped us. As in Kate's experience, asking God for help is often our last resort. We know we need to change, but we do not know how.

Another reason why we encourage people to hear the voice of the Lord talking to them about themselves is hinted at by Derry. There is in some of our churches a prejudice against *everyone* hearing the Lord's voice directly. We see this prejudice in our expectation that our leaders will hear God for us. After all, they are the mature ones, educated to hear God's voice, and don't we pay them to do this? Such an attitude means that, in part at least, we pass over to others the responsibility for our spiritual well-being. We become passive about our

Christian journey, relying on others and in some ways allowing our spiritual experience of the Lord to be second-hand. We see this attitude in the large number of people waiting to see the pastor, or our talking about the spiritual adventures of others rather than about our own. When we are willing to hear the voice of the Lord for ourselves, talking to us about us, we begin to be more responsible for our own faith walk. We begin to rely less on others and on what they think is wrong with us, focusing instead on how the Lord views us, with all our baggage and history.

One final reason for emphasizing your need to hear the voice of the Lord for yourself is our common and stubborn refusal to change. Few of us instinctively take responsibility for ourselves, because we live in a culture where others sort us out and tell us what we must do. Our whole western culture is much like our church culture, in which we are passive observers. So for many of us it will take a dramatic shift for us to begin believing we can change our ways and help ourselves, by accepting we could become more than we already are. But first we must accept that we are currently not the person God intended we should be, and we need to hear His view of us if we are to change. We must allow Him to lead this process.

Some of us would respond by saying it is easy to accept the fact that Derry heard God's voice. After all, he'd been a Christian for years. But what about Kate? She didn't have a relationship with God when she came to us for help. But her story suggests she started hearing God's voice before she became a Christian. In our work we have watched God introduce Himself to many people, whilst He is in the process of helping them become more whole. He never presses them to make a decision to follow Him. He just begins to talk to them, helping them become more who they were created to be, letting them discover Him along the way. With many who do not know God, we teach them, like Kate, to begin listening to their inner voice – not the voices in their heads, but the kind of voice Kate always had with her.

One of the most interesting points Derry made about hearing God's voice was the way he had elevated his mind and intellect, and by doing so had all but eliminated the possibility of engaging spiritual reality. Did you notice what he said when Peter first talked to him about his fear? His mind didn't understand the comment, but to his surprise he started weeping. Engaging historic emotion is often God's 'second chance' for us to sort out the kind of thing that both Derry and Kate had done in suppressing their feelings. The Hebrew view of emotion is that all feelings have both a good and a bad side, e.g. love can be healthy or manipulative; anger can be righteous or unrighteous, as can any feeling. We must allow the Lord to talk to us about the way we have abused our emotion and our feelings. We must begin to say sorry, by allowing the Holy Spirit to bring to the surface all our repressed toxic painful feelings, so we can give these feelings to the Lord. He helps to teach us how we can change our emotional life.

Notes

1 We work with many people who have suffered extreme self-hate. They are used to 'beating themselves up' with words and thoughts. Kate is describing the 'voice' of her human spirit, the God-breathed part of her, speaking love and affirmation of who He created her to be.

2 We encourage people, with the Lord's help, to use their imagination in a godly way as part of their journey. It's one of

the ways God uses to bring significant healing to us, for He cannot take from us what we do not first emotionally own.

[3] In our work we encourage people to say sorry to the Lord for specific areas of damage in their lives, either before or as they discover them. These detailed acts of repentance give God the opportunity to begin speaking to us about the damage and bring us deeper healing.

[4] We refer quite a lot in our work to the human spirit and to our emotions. It is a part of our human nature that is referred to many times in Scripture. See for example Genesis 1-2 and Psalm 51. For a good book introducing the subject, sadly now only available second-hand, see Come, A.B., *Human Spirit and Holy Spirit* (Philadelphia: Westminster Press, 1959).

[5] This is a very common problem, when a person is physically present but not emotionally present. You somehow sense that they are absent, they are somewhere else. In our mentor training we help people to learn how to be present when one is trying to help them.

[6] Being present to yourself means that you are at ease in body and spirit, you enjoy being who you are and you do not want to escape, run away or disconnect.

2

New Careers

At the heart of our community is a simple principle – that
if you are growing in your relationship with Christ, you
will also be growing in wholeness. Or if you are growing
in wholeness, you will also be growing in your potential
for intimacy with Christ. It seems obvious. God wants to
give us a fulfilling life, so that His grace and favour will
fill all we are becoming. The Lord God wants to help us
know Him better, while we also become more whole. On
this basis, He will want us to sort out areas of damage or
baggage that we may carry, because they stand in the
path of His relationship with us.[1] For instance, if we have
had bad experiences of fathering or have been abused by
men, this will colour our attitude to Father God, or the
man Christ. Alternatively, if we have known only failure,
or have experienced trauma or abuse in our lives, we will
not want to take further risks that make us vulnerable,
even with God helping us.

We take this principle of God wanting to help us even
further, focusing on our personal responsibility to
cooperate with Him in our own wholeness. To be whole,
we cannot be passive. For instance, in Exodus 15:26 we

find a conditional promise from the Lord. *'If you listen carefully to the voice of the Lord your God and do what is right in his eyes, if you pay attention to his commands and keep all his decrees, I will not bring on you any of the diseases I brought on the Egyptians. I am the Lord, who heals you.'*

This early promise of the Lord states that we need to hear His voice and then do what He says. The suggestion in this text, as in others in Scripture (e.g. Deuteronomy 28:58-60), is that if we obey Him and live in this way, letting God heal us, we will not suffer like those who are disobedient to Him.[2] Hearing His voice and acting on it is a fundamental requirement for deepening intimacy with Christ, as well as for our moving into personal and relational wholeness.

This healing is available to Christian and non-Christian alike (note Jesus' own ministry, healing all who came to Him, not just those who followed Him). So we can welcome onto this journey both the Kates and the Derrys of this world. Our experience is that many who don't know Jesus will in time want to know Him, as they begin to discover the reality of Him making them whole. They will want to meet the God who is healing them. What Kate and Derry were learning, and what we all learn doing this journey, is that God is more eager to talk to us about the baggage He sees standing between us and Him than we are willing to give the time and energy to doing something about it.

In acting in this way we are taking up the simple principle that Christ has a heart to help all of us become the person He created us to be, before He requires that we serve Him. So within CCD and *Rapha* we are first and foremost passionately committed to loving and helping people, caring for them and supporting them on their journey towards more wholeness. Then, at some point on their journey they will freely choose to begin more directly to love and serve Christ in their wholeness.

When Christ brings wholeness to us, it is very noticeable. Even those who do not know about your previous need will see the change in you. We could have chosen from many stories of people in the community and *Rapha* who have found this type of greater wholeness, as well as a deepening relationship with God. The combination leads to remarkably changed lives. We'd like to introduce you to two folk, Rebecca and John. Note the way that their willingness to pursue wholeness meant they could meet Jesus, and in a relatively short period of time were experiencing significant personal redemption.

Possessing My Dream
Rebecca Mitchell

I'm 39 and got married last year to Steve. I have two boys, Alistair (12) and Harry (10), and Steve's daughter Rebecca (16) also lives with us. I've lived in Deal all my life. Christ Church is the first church I've been part of. I joined five years ago. I love seeing people change. I get a buzz from seeing how they come alive after being in a hard place.

When I was at school, in my fifth year, we had work experience and I chose to go to a local probation office, because I wanted to be a probation officer. But then I decided that I wasn't intelligent enough to go to college or university to pursue that dream. This was all tied up with my mum pushing me to do well at school, and she had her reasons, but out of revenge against her, I chose to muck up. So I left school and did dead-end jobs. I was an accounts clerk, a hotel receptionist, a bus driver, and I worked on the Channel ferries. Later, when my boys from my first marriage were old enough to go to school, I got a job at a residential home for adults with challenging behaviour, learning difficulties and mental health problems.

I started off as a carer and then became an assistant coordinator for the clients' activities and later the coordinator. That involved organizing their day from about 8:30 in the morning to about 5:30 at night. It could be college, counselling, sports, anything they would like to do. I decided to take a new approach. Whereas before everybody did the same activity together, and there were so many instances of people not wanting to do it, I decided that I would change their day programme to meet their own needs, so they had choices. And it worked very well. If they became grumpy and said, 'I'm not gonna do it,' I could say, 'Well, it was your choice and we have staff for you and we'd like you to go,' rather than 'You will go to the activity that we want you to go to.' So it did stop quite a lot of the bad behaviour and that was good. I really enjoyed my time there and I still miss the clients even now – they were great. I'd got as far as wanting to do something that was about caring for people, without the need to get lots of qualifications.

But personally, I was going through a terrible time. My partner Steve and I had split up. We'd been together for about three years, although they were horrendous, a nightmare, because of my past, because of his past. At the time he used alcohol to cope, which added to the pressure, so it wasn't a good start. Also, I was massively in debt. I felt depressed to the point where it was so bad that I wanted to give the boys back to their father because I didn't feel I could look after them. I didn't want to do that, but I couldn't see another way. I was in despair and had no hope.

That was when I spoke to a member of staff who was from Christ Church. I knew there was something about this guy that was different, and I knew that whatever he had I wanted. He was great; he just used to let me talk. One day he said, 'I think there are some people that can help you.' He said it was a church that he had joined. But I carried such shame and guilt, blaming myself for my marriage break-up, for the boys' not having a father, for all the wrong decisions I'd made. I thought that if I went to church people they would feel that I was a terrible mother, or a terrible person, and I didn't want to put myself through that. That was how I perceived church – you're bad, you're terrible, go confess your sins. At first I said, 'No, thank you,' but in the end it got so bad that I knew I had to do something. So when he invited me to Christ Church's Christmas celebration, I welcomed the opportunity to go.

I took the boys along to the hall they were using. The whole place was lit up with little candles and everyone was singing carols, and the people were lovely. I was expecting to be hounded by people carrying Bibles under their arms, but it wasn't like that. The boys had a great time. The children were running around freely and enjoying themselves, and nobody tutted or groaned. The boys said, 'Can we come again, Mum?' I decided that if the boys felt they enjoyed it, then OK, I'd go. So I went there for a month, just on Sunday, sitting in the back row, being there but pretending not to be there, just chatting to people. But then, listening to the teaching one Sunday, I thought I'd ring and ask if it was possible to have a chat with Susan and Peter.

When I got there, I thought they would sort my problems out. I would just go along and it would be all right. They agreed they would help me, but said that I was the one who was going to have to sort my problems out. I realized I was going to have to take responsibility. They asked me if I would like to do the journey without God, since I didn't have a church background. I was frightened to death of God because I thought he would condemn me for who I was. So I agreed, 'I'll do it by myself, thank you.' But I went on an Introductory Workshop and realized God didn't judge me. I found the religious side quite difficult, mainly because I didn't have any church background, but I did grasp the principles of

Changed Lives

the journey. My eyes just opened. I realized there was a reason why I felt the way I did. I wasn't mad, after all, and I wasn't this green-eyed monster that I thought I was.

I had thought I was odd and different. As we have a lot of mental illness within the family, I had almost assumed I was going to end up in an institution like all of them. So to have people within the church who were honest in saying, 'This is how I'm feeling' was amazing, because among the people I'd been around till then, nobody would say what they were feeling. They'd pretend that everything in the garden was rosy and their lives were all sorted and it was fine, which left me thinking, 'It must be just me.' And then to be shown the tools, how to let go of your feelings and give them to God and move forward, was, well, the key to the door. I didn't need to do it on my own after all. So I started my homework journey, with God.

But let me go back to a point about six months into my journey, when I was really struggling with the wrong decisions I'd made in my past. I had thought I'd made them because I didn't have a choice, but I now see that was a lie. I did have a choice. I chose to make those decisions. At the time, however, I'd thought I was trapped in a corner. So by leaving school and deciding not to go to college I'd set myself up, betrayed myself. I had been in the A band at school. There was no reason for me to believe that I wasn't intelligent enough. I was so sorry for what I'd done to myself. I'd basically mucked up for twenty years. And my mentor said, 'OK, you mucked up. But what if you could change anything now, what would you want to be?'[3] It was at that point that I said, 'I want to be a probation officer.' Six months later an advertisement appeared in the paper. I knew that's who I'd wanted to be, and I had not become her. So it was as if

God was saying, 'OK, you couldn't be her then. How about being her now?'

I knew it was what I wanted, so I decided to apply. But I didn't get the application form in time. I thought, 'Oh, OK, it's not meant to be,' and just left it. And then a year later I was actually invited to re-apply. Oh, wow! That was the first of many 'Oh, wow!' moments. I wasn't even actively thinking about this job any more – the letter just arrived on the doorstep.

The application form was absolutely massive, with lots of different sections. They included, 'How do you solve problems within the workplace and how do you break them down? How do you work as a team member and how do you work within an organization? How do you value diversity?' And I was thinking, 'I don't know, I just do it. If there's a problem at work, I just solve it.' I got in touch with my friend and mentor. She and I often walk when we're struggling with stuff. We walk from Deal to St Margaret's and back, which is about six miles each way. So we walked all the way to St Margaret's and she was saying to me, 'When there's a problem at work, what do you do?' 'Well, I just sort it out.' She enabled me to break it down into little steps. 'Somebody is not feeling that brilliant. How can you see that from their behaviour, and what do you do because of that? Do you take them out of the situation or do you wait? And why did you decide that?' I began to realize, 'Oh, that's why I do it, and that's how I do it!' So by the time we got back to Deal, I could fill out the application form.

Next, I had to go for a day's assessment in Brighton. This was really scary. We had to do a time management exercise, summarize a paper, demonstrate group work skills and deliver a presentation. The presentation was about a violent incident at work and how I managed it. I felt comfortable about doing that because it was based on my relationship with clients, but that would come at the end of the day. The first exercise was about time management, not one of my strongest points. It involved a diary and some e-mails and at that point, because I wasn't computer-friendly, I didn't even know what an e-mail was. Does an e-mail mean it's really important? Or do I just have to read the e-mail and see if it's important? We had to read all our e-mails, make our diary, prioritize a week and give reasons. So I thought, 'But I don't know how to do this. I can't do this. I'm just going to go home now.'

There was a big window in the room where we were working. I looked out to the sea and silently said to God, 'I can't do this. You've got to help me. I can't do it.' And I just looked back at the paper and found I could do it. Everything had become clear. The fear had gone. 'You can do it, Rebecca, it's all right.' And I found it quite easy, once I'd come out of the fear. The fear had so nearly overwhelmed me, but now I knew that God was sitting there with me. 'It's OK, you know you can do it.' So I did it. And I did the exercise on summarizing a paper – I just did it.

Then came the group work exercise and there were some very strong characters, people with strong opinions, within the group. What I had found in the past was that if I came across people like them I would close down. But there was this guiding voice saying, 'No, Rebecca, your opinion is valued. You can talk it out, it's all right, and even if you get it wrong it doesn't matter, just say how you feel.' So that was good too, and then the presentation went really well. I had passed the day's assessment.

The next stage was an interview with a panel of people, and I was able to answer their questions. But then there was a question that I misunderstood. What I said in reply was obviously not relevant to the question, so the guy said to me, 'You have not answered the question!' I could have lost myself then, but I thought, 'Don't do it, Rebecca, don't do it. Just think, "OK, I made a mistake, now wait for the next question."'

The very next day someone rang me at work and said, 'The meeting that you went to yesterday . . .' But I hadn't been at a meeting yesterday. I thought the call was work-related, and then she said, 'We'd like to offer you the job.' They'd offered me the job! I was a trainee probation officer, beginning to achieve my lifelong dream. My prayer had been answered.

That was the easiest bit! Then I was training for two years, working as a trainee probation officer, but within those two years I had to gain a BA Hons in Criminal Justice Studies and a National Vocational Qualification (NVQ) Level Four in Community Justice. Once again I was thinking, 'I can't do this.' I worked four days a week, and I had over an hour's travel to and from my work placement. Then there was my home and my family. We had one study day a week and we had to complete the degree in a year. It was distance learning. So in other words, we were just given books and had to go away and read them, then write an essay. I had no idea where to start. Work for the NVQ was built around gathering evidence of our professional practice: this is how I did it, this is how I didn't do it, and this is what I learnt from it. I could do that now.

A particularly hard part for me was having to produce a manual in relation to a group work programme. The wording was very academic, so I had to read it, try to understand it, then put what was said in simple terms and deliver it to the individuals. As I presented it, I thought they would be judging me, because I had already judged myself and decided that I wasn't any good. So I was making a complete hash of it. I went to see Susan. 'I can't deliver this material, I don't understand it.' She said, 'It's not the material, Rebecca. You deliver to groups in church, so why is this so different?' It was because the people in church loved me, and I loved them, so I felt comfortable. That's why it was different. So what I decided to do was to pretend that each person I was delivering the manual to was somebody within the church. I went in with that mindset, did it, and passed. That was another hurdle overcome.

Trainee probation officers are under the supervision of a senior probation officer within the workplace. Mine trained me to write reports, to do the paper work, to try to manage my time better, talking through my cases and anything I was struggling with. More than that, she really believed I could do the job. I needed that, because at the time I struggled to believe in myself. 'If you believe in yourself, Rebecca, you can do this job,' she told me. 'You've got so many skills with the offenders. You work well with them. You can learn paperwork, forms, computers and all the other stuff – I don't have to teach you people skills, so all you've got to worry about is managing the mounds of paper, and not being so hard on yourself.' She was great.

But I was struggling to believe in myself because of the self-hate that I carried. I believed the lie that I would not be able to achieve any of it, gain the degree, do the NVQ, do the group skills, do the court work, write the reports. Without the support of God and the Christ Church community there's no way this could have happened, because I wanted to bin it so many times.

During my training, I'd just get the hang of something and the difficulty would go up another level. I simply felt that it was beyond me. I felt I couldn't do it. But every time I reached that point and I said to God, 'I can't do this. I have no more capacity – it's just blank – there's nothing there,' he'd always say, 'It's OK, Rebecca, you can do it.' Each time when I've doubted myself, I've asked God for help and then realized that I can do it!

So what am I hoping for? What do I want in the future, in the next few years of this new career? Recently a senior colleague thanked me for being so supportive of my colleagues in the workplace. She said, 'You've only been here a little while, but you look out for people and know when they're not feeling good. You support them through those times, even though you have enough of your own work. . . . It's been noticed.' She then said she would like to see me become a Practice Teacher, training trainee probation officers, or become a senior member of a case management team, developing team members.

To enable me to develop my teaching skills, I would love to learn to teach the *Rapha* principles in workshops around the world, giving others hope that they can change. Another area I would like to work in, in some way, would be alongside individuals with learning difficulties, to enable them to change and reach their potential.

Nobody said anything about fast track. And that's how it feels with my journey at the moment. I used to know where I was going. I was going to let go of my past and have a future, and I've been able to do that. So now I'm professionally qualified and Steve and I are married. We have a home and a family, and life is great. It's fantastic – so this feels like the scary bit in a way, because everything is going really well. Now it's as if God's saying, 'You're now a probation officer. Congratulations, but I now want you to do much more.' This is amazing, but it's also very scary because part of me just wants to plod along now, yet I know there's more.

I think of mentoring and leading a group as a sort of hobby. Within Christ Church we mentor each other, under the guidance of the Leadership Team. I lead a discipleship group, and I love being there for the other ladies and encouraging them to support and be there for each other. Within the group we make declarations of where we want to be in the future, and who we want to become. We review our declarations every three months, and if people are struggling we ask the Lord to show them what's stopping them, what's getting in the way. It's all very positive, because there's a goal at the end and nine times out of ten they will reach that goal. Then it's on to the next goal, and the next.

Yes, life was hard five years ago, but with God, the Christ Church community and the *Rapha* teaching, life is now amazing. I have been able to let go of the lies I believed about myself in the past. I now have a future and my dream. I have been able to support others through difficult times, and I am a professional person. Before this, I was a single parent who was struggling and had no hope. Then I found answers to my questions, saw light at the end of the tunnel, and have never looked back. The future is where I now look. I love my job, I am married, the kids are doing just fine and I want to give hope to all those I meet. If you want to change, you can; it does not have to be the way it is. The past steals your future, but letting go of it enables you to become free, to stop believing the lies you think about yourself. You do not have to carry them, you are able to make your own choices: nothing stops you. The world is your oyster: take both hands and grab what is rightfully yours.

Life Change, Career Change
John Flicker

I'm 36, single, and I was born in Mile End, East London. I've just ended a relationship of eleven years. I moved to Deal to join the church nearly three years ago. I enjoy spending time with my daughter Emy (9) and playing football.

So how did I get onto this journey of discovery and healing? It was becoming a Christian that brought me to Deal, but only indirectly. I became a Christian five or six years ago. My life was a mess. Things were really bad at work and really bad in my relationship with my girlfriend at the time, Caroline, the mother of my daughter. Also, my mum and dad were in hospital and my daughter wasn't well. Life was just a nightmare.

Caroline had been a Christian for about six months and she put it to me that the only way for our relationship to go forward would be if I became a Christian. And so, because part of me loved her so much, out of my need, my baggage, my feelings of 'I can't live life without her,' I was willing to go along with what she wanted. I went to a few church meetings and I did come out of one of them crying. I started crying on my own because these people looked so happy and I wanted to be happy.

Then one day, I was driving along thinking about how bad everything was with my daughter, with my mum and dad in hospital, and with Caroline. I was angry, I was hurting, and I actually cried out to God. I swore at Him along the lines of, 'If you're really out there and you really care, now's your chance,' and just as I said that, a van drove in front of me and it had written on it John 8:32: 'You shall know the truth, and the truth shall set you free.' And with that came such a feeling of euphoria that I was just overcome. I started crying and screaming at the top of my voice. I just didn't know what was going on, but somewhere in all of that was the feeling that everything was going to be all right. I phoned Caroline's mother: 'Christine, I don't know what's happened but I think I've found God.' I was crying my eyes out all afternoon. It wasn't sad crying; it was a kind of happy crying, with me saying, 'I think I've found God' over and over.

When I got home that night Caroline was very different. My mum and dad came out of hospital on the same day, and things were just fine. For about six months I was a mad evangelical guy who would say, 'Jesus. You need Jesus,' and 'God is this,' and 'God is that.' But after about six months I was having to admit that nothing had changed. I still got the same feelings, I still hated the world, and now I was beginning to hate people in church. Hate, hate, hate. Everything around me was the same as it had been six months before – nothing had changed. And I was thinking, 'It doesn't work – it's starting not to work now.' I didn't blame God really – there was no talking to God. I'd had this dramatic experience and it had kept me going for six months. Now what was I supposed to do?

My relationship with my girlfriend was still a mess, we were still fighting and arguing, so we went to see the pastor. The advice we were given was, 'Go away and pray about it.' What do we pray? We could read the Bible and it was just another story. It didn't mean anything. Then we went to loads of other churches, Christian camps and conferences. While they were great religious experiences, there was nothing life-changing about any of this for either of us. A lot of things were happening for other people, but not for us. For us it was just a shambles, a mess.

I gave up Christianity. It didn't work because I didn't know God. I didn't know anybody. But since coming down to Deal, I've found out more about me by doing this journey. I've found out more about how I've actually lived and the false picture I'd contrived, instead of admitting how life was. I can now see that the other churches I went to had no idea how to handle someone like me.

Now, before I go on, I need to tell you what I mean. You see, I used to be someone who did jobs that were baggage-related, for example as a bodyguard to the Saudi and Qatari royal families. I was an enforcer for local criminals who wanted money collected. These jobs put me in the firing line, feeding my self-hate and self-destructive tendencies. They were dead-end jobs, with no promotion, no security, done solely for the money I could get at the time. I was a criminal, a working-class criminal who didn't deserve anything but a working-class criminal's life with its poverty, stress and illness, and all the other things that go with it.

I was a thuggish guy. What I'm about to say might seem odd, but I was a very good drug dealer. I was very good at handling people and very good at dealing with money. I was an armed robber, which meant being able to think on my feet and being very practical. I now realize these were all transferable skills! They were good skills in the wrong context. So I've always known that whatever I did, I was good at it. But I never actually felt good about me. The skills that I had never amounted to anything; it was always disappointment after disappointment after disappointment. God and the church were about to be another disappointment.

Caroline's mum, Christine, went on a *Rapha* Introductory Workshop and came back and told Caroline about it. Later Caroline went on a workshop, and came back and told me. By this time I had had enough of Christianity. It was a load of rubbish and never worked. But in the end Caroline persuaded me. I came expecting nothing. I was here in Deal to fill time. The first session of the weekend began. Peter came out and started talking, and within five or ten minutes I realized he had something to say. By the end of the workshop I knew my life was a mess: not yet how much of a mess, but I knew this guy could help.

We were taught about something called homework.[4] So I went away and started doing homework for about six weeks, or what I thought was homework, but then I just went back to my old ways. At this time I was a drug dealer, but feeling a conflict: I wanted to do the right thing but I was also selling drugs. So when things got really bad, I'd phone a couple of times and speak to Peter or I'd come down and speak to him. Then he suggested I should come to the meetings that were held on Tuesday nights for the men of the church. So I'd drive down from London. I stuck to that for about six weeks. I started to do homework again, but I realized that I was only taking the edge off my life. My lifestyle was piling up on me: I was doing Deal on the Tuesday night, taking the lid off so I could survive, and then after six weeks I would go back to my old ways until it got really bad again. Then I'd come down and speak to Peter and then I'd do it again. I did that for about a year, and then the following November, exactly one year after doing the first workshop, I came down to do another one. After that, I knew I had to move to Deal and become part of Christ Church full-time. Caroline also moved down to Deal with our daughter, and now we're in regular contact, although we're not living together.

Here at Christ Church, 'church' isn't just about Sunday morning. For the other churches I'd been to, the main thrust was Sunday morning. There was the hour on Sunday morning, the cup of tea afterwards, clearing up then going home, and perhaps a group on a Tuesday or a Wednesday night. In Deal it's much more life-oriented. We actually associate and do things all through the week with people from the church. It's not compartmentalized into 'religious' and 'everything else'. Church is about being in relationship with yourself and with others. And so it's about relationships, it's about living, it's about life, and there is attention to the practicalities of how to help people, rather than just the abstract 'Go away and pray.' I didn't find that in the other churches. Since I've come down here, Christianity has not been a shambles. It has worked and continues to work.

The last three years have been the hardest of my life, but also the most enjoyable. I'm on a journey from being what I thought I had to be, without choices, to being the person I want to become. I am now in transition. I've never known job satisfaction. But now, on this journey, I am finding more of myself, finding out more about relationships and people. I've had to learn that there is more to life than earning money and spending money. I'm clearing out the hate and discovering the potential of who I really am.

Two years ago I started thinking I wanted to go to university. It was because of the change in me. Doing this journey has made me realize that the more I relate to myself, the better person I can be, with myself and with others. There is no distinction between going to university, being a better father, being a good friend to people, and just being a good friend to myself. Just to look at getting to university would be to take away from the journey itself, because university is an outworking of the 'me being me' journey, part of a wider thing. I don't think just going to university would have solved any problems in itself, even if I could have got myself there, thinking the way I used to. There had to be an outworking of problems and an outworking of how I feel about myself. I couldn't go to university until I had dealt with issues about 'me' going to university, about 'me' being John, about 'me' doing anything, really.

My new career is going to be about me wanting to be me, and that's something I've never wanted to be before. I've never wanted to be me, because I grew up expecting people to hurt me. I went around with my mates; we were a gang of friends, a bunch of brothers. The reason we went around together was because we didn't have anyone else. It's hard to explain, but we got from each other what we didn't get from anyone else. We watched out for each other. We needed each other. I've been told since that they looked to me for leadership. They thought I was fearless and yet all the time I was actually full of fear.

Even while doing a one-year Access to Higher Education course I never actually believed that I could go to university. I went to college for a year, one night a week and one morning a week, doing the Access course, as well as working. I finished that in mid-June and applied to the university in September. When I spoke to the university about doing a degree, there were loads of obstacles in my way, and each obstacle just reminded me that I didn't really deserve to be there.

I got the university application forms and one of the questions was, 'Have you got a criminal record?' My criminal record is quite extensive and violent, including robbery, theft and malicious wounding, but I didn't have any offences that actually excluded me from doing a degree, which are sex offences and arson. Before the university would accept me I had to get a letter from the Probation Office to say that I wasn't a sex offender and I hadn't committed arson, and all the time there was no place for me at the university, which was reinforcing my belief that I didn't deserve to be there. It was all going to be for nothing, and I was just wasting my time.

But there are two sides to it. There's the side of me that says, 'No, I'm not listening to that,' and then there's the side that says, 'Yeah, you ain't worth it, you haven't got anything to give, you're a total failure.' And I could hear in these voices echoes of what my dad had always said to me: 'You're useless, you're never gonna be nuffink,' and so it went on for four or five weeks. The Probation Service was kind of helpful, but unhelpful, saying I had to send them a letter giving permission for them to give the university information about me. It was going on and on, sending me into trauma: 'Is it really worth it?' If I really believed in myself, I could do what I wanted without a degree, couldn't I? But for me now a degree is a measure of who I am, and it's the first part of what I want to do.

Finally I got to the point where they offered me an interview, but I still carried the idea that I didn't actually deserve a place at the university. That is what I carried into the interview and I am sure now that is what came through, to be picked up by the interviewing panel: that part of me didn't actually want the place at the university. That's the sort of thing I'd been doing to myself all my life. I got a letter saying there was no place for me.

That sent me into serious trauma. Again I contemplated leaving the church. It was all a load of rubbish and I didn't deserve to be part of it. This was just another

Christian shambles. Then I spoke to Peter and he persuaded me to go back to the university and fight for my place, to see the people I needed to see and talk to them about it, rather than just sit down, grin and bear it and give up. So I went back to the allocation officer and explained to him that over the year of the Access course I had consistently had the highest marks in the class, and that people with far lower marks had already been accepted. Within a day, I got the e-mail telling me there was a place. All I had to do was provide evidence from the work I'd done, and I was in.

And now it's one year on, and I've just heard I got a 2:1 for my first year. I've learnt a lot about the subject, obviously, but also about me. I now realize I could have done far, far better than I did, and I'm looking forward to the next year and actually sitting down and doing it, and getting even more satisfaction out of doing it than I've ever had before. I know I will get that now. For the second and third years I'm really going to do what I need to do to get it done. And that will facilitate the rest of my academic career.

Just going to university has opened me up to a whole new way of living. I don't have to be contrived at university: I can just be me. In every other place I've ever been, prison for example, I've always had to contrive 'me', so as to keep safe, to keep alive, and I don't have to do that at university. It's a place I actually love going to. And I do deserve to be there.

As for the future, I'd like to do a PhD. Then I would just become an expert in whatever field I choose to pursue, and see how I go on from there . . . write a few books . . . see what happens. But that's not just a dream, 'Oh, one day I'll write a book.' No, I can write a book, quite seriously. It's not that far away. It's not an unrealistic goal. It's quite a realistic goal. I can do this!

But going to university is just one strand of me finding me. Part of that has been getting into relationships with others, and when I say relationships I mean deeper relationships, relationships that really count, which means making myself vulnerable with people. I'm just beginning to open myself up and be willing to take the risk of doing relationships, and I'm not going to run away any more. This is a journey that I have to stay on.

Now I can actually sit down and say, 'Look, my life is a mess.' Even though I now know a lot more of myself than I've ever known, there's still a mess and there's still some way to go to sort it out, but I could never go back to being the person I was. That's just impossible to do.

The outworking of that change shows in my relationships with my daughter and with my new housemates. I can begin to be me more often. I can be me, more than not being me. I'm able now to take responsibility for what's happened, and I'm able to go into relationships not with a need, but with a desire. I want to be there *for the other person*. I find out who I am more and more, and by doing that I can give more and more of myself, and no longer out of need.

Some Comments

These two fascinating stories are repeated many times throughout Christ Church and *Rapha*. We have found that when God starts bringing healing, it impacts every area of our lives. So we see that our toxic history is like tramlines and, if we allow it to, it will also dictate our future. But God wants to change this, to stop us fulfilling the intent of our baggage. Under normal circumstances most of us are cursed to repeat the damage and consequences of our parents' actions. Instead, with God's help we are able to break these cycles and expect levels of change in all areas of our life, as a direct fruit of our healing journey. This is the norm in our community – to see significant positive change, over a period of time. Instant change is not trusted.

You will have noticed that both Rebecca and John had really low opinions of themselves. They were both living the way they felt they deserved. These feelings were so deeply rooted that in John's case they were about to drive him away from his relationship with God. Trying to receive God's love while hating oneself so deeply creates an intolerable conflict that just serves to make us all the more angry, leading to further failure. So as part of the response to this we teach people to begin looking at themselves from God's perspective, rather than from the perspective of their damaged past. It allows us all to let go of the lies which in the past we have believed about ourselves, and begin seeing ourselves as God does.

For both Rebecca and John the workshops played a key role. They both suddenly realized there were specific reasons for all the failure and betrayal in their histories. Such truth and its knowledge, when released to the person, can be life-transforming. They can do something about their problems. So the key truth in this chapter is that you are not trapped, you are not cursed with having to live the same old ways for the rest of your life. God is offering an alternative that with your co-operation will allow you to break with the humdrum of the past and to own a new future, learning to possess your dreams.

Having said that, we do not believe God has created a blueprint of who we should become, some kind of route-map. To have such a fixed plan already set for us would be counter to the way God is: He has given us personal free will. Also, we do not see this new way of living and being as something like a tightrope which God expects us to find and then walk along. Instead we would see God giving each of us a unique cocktail of gifts and abilities, natural and supernatural, that we can make what we like of. But He knows that if we possess all He has given us, making it our own within allegiance to Christ, we will live significant lives both for Him and for ourselves.

The community and the workshops offer a set of tools allowing an individual to begin this journey of change. But these changes will not only happen because God acts supernaturally. They will happen because both you and God work really hard to realize all the future potential in new ways. Healing brings an empowering, an ability to do good for yourself, making decisions for positive change rather than remaining a passive spectator of other people's successes. Moving into these new areas without doing the homework first would be impossible.

Notes

[1] Baggage is the word we use to describe the accumulated damage in each of our lives. In essence it could be described as sin, because for many of us it is our refusal to change our ways, despite the damage we may be continuing to do to ourselves by our refusal to change.

[2] Psalm 103:3 and Mark 1:34, among many others, also demonstrate the life we can enjoy when we obey His conditions for our healing and do as He requires.

[3] One of our therapeutic practices in Christ Church is to encourage people to choose someone to act as an empathic friend, a mentor, who can offer support on the discipleship journey, drawing on their own personal experience.

[4] Homework is the term we use to describe the discipline of giving regular blocks of time to allow the Lord to talk to us, and for us to learn how to respond in a positive way by looking at the reasons why we do not want to change.

3

Womanhood

Both John's and Rebecca's stories in the previous chapter illustrate how much our past can steal from our future. Neither of them would have been able to move into their growing wholeness without undoing their histories. And John is quite clear that his experience of Christianity was going to collapse if he didn't find a way of undoing the damage of his history.

This is a fundamental principle in our community and workshop teaching. We see the gaining of more wholeness as a journey, step by step, working through one area of damage from our history at a time. As we begin to hear the Lord's voice talking to us about us, He will set the agenda, unpacking our toxic history in an ordered way, as He sees fit. This is often likened by folk to the defusing of a bomb. It needs to be done in the correct way, unique to each of us.

Others find helpful the analogy of our spiritual and emotional life being like a spiritual house. We enter the hallway early on, but it is only with the Lord's help that we can enter each room and begin cleaning up one after the other. Each room will have a name over the locked door, saying things like 'mother', 'father', 'abuse', 'manhood', 'career', 'self-harm', etc. Each step forward opens up the way for the next. All the windows will be open to the Enemy or anyone who wants to come in and spoil our lives, but without the Lord's help we cannot get in, close the windows or begin to clean up the room. For many of us, the destination of the journey will be to fully occupy all the rooms of our house. This will be maturity; this will be wholeness.

The next two stories introduce what this principle meant for two women. Nicola is a member of the community here in Deal. When she joined us she was an experienced Christian, having served the Lord full-time with her husband, and was unaware of any areas of need in her life. Her husband was the one with the problem! Norma lives in Oregon, USA. She is a member of Derry's congregation and Derry first asked us to meet her when she was physically very sick. She then attended our workshops. These two women have walked very different journeys, but there are a number of similar principles. They have sought to discover their own unique womanhood in Christ.

Both Nicola and Norma refer to the *Gender Continuum*. This is a simple tool to help anyone discover how male or female they really are. In diagram form (see below) it is a horizontal line representing both male and female. We bisect this line vertically at the centre, with the left side being female, the right side being male. Everyone is somewhere on the horizontal line. All men will be on the male side of the line, although some may be closer to the centre, demonstrating more 'female' skills and preferences. Likewise all women will be on the female side of the line, although some may be closer to 'male', moving towards the centre of the line, in their skills and preferences. Everyone starts as a dot on either the male or

female side of the line. But I propose to them that Christ
represents the whole line, as an example for both male
and female. Likewise, maturity and wholeness in Christ,
the fruit of one's personal journey, means you will
become the whole line of your gender, either male or
female. We have also developed a gender questionnaire
that helps people locate themselves on the line. This
Gender Continuum is a particularly beneficial concept for
those believing they are trapped in unhelpful gender
stereotyping.

Woman		Man	
Very Female	Female with male mind	Male with female mind	Very Male

Welcoming Womanhood
Nicola Carnall

I'm 40 years old and married to Martin, with two children, Michael (9) and Deborah (8). I was born in Deal and have been going to church for most of my life. I joined Christ Church shortly after it was started. I don't have much time for hobbies, but have discovered I'm really good at figures and am just completing a Diploma in Management.

I think what happened was that as I was growing up I didn't fit into the mould. I thought I should, but actually I was too different. When I was about 8 I threw all my dolls and soft toys away and started to ask for cars. But it wasn't until I was 11 that my mother gave me these things. I really needed toys that 'did things', like construction kits that I could make, remake and change.

I spent a lot of my life thinking that there was something wrong with me, that I wasn't who I should be. That was my view of myself. It was the sin I did against myself.[1] But it was also partly what I'd learnt from others: that the person I was wasn't acceptable.

But after I'd met the person God had created me to be I knew she was OK. There were areas of her I had been reluctant to explore, because they didn't fit with my view, my mother's view or other family members' views of who I should be. So it stopped me understanding womanhood.

I was a tomboy at primary school. In secondary school I became a loner. My mum found me difficult to buy for, because she couldn't buy the 'nice dresses', the latest 'whatever' that the other girls were into – I wasn't there. While my sister Lucinda asked to borrow £2 for a pair of ballet shoes, I asked for £2 for a pair of hockey boots. I grew up with the sense that I just didn't fit. I viewed my difference as unacceptable, but doing this journey I have come to realize I was mocked a lot in my family because I was different. I had this view of what a woman should be, probably from quite early on. I never dreamt of getting married and I never wanted to cook.

I started coming back to church when I was about 16, and in church there was a particular view of women. So for me, a woman was someone who could make the house lovely, cook for twenty extra people if they turned up, care for children, create sticky, gluey stuff with the kids, and so on. So when I went on the first *Rapha* womanhood workshop I approached it with fear and trepidation, expecting it to be about becoming this certain type of woman. I just knew I was going to fail. I already hated myself, so I thought, 'Well, I'm already useless, good for nothing, because I don't measure up.'

At the beginning of the workshop they were talking about loving yourself, but I couldn't. Then they began talking about the *Gender Continuum*, and we did a questionnaire.

Afterwards, talking with the ladies, I found out where other people were. There I was, right down at the male end of female, while some of my friends were in the middle, a bit female, and at the other end women who were into things like dance, babies and interior decor. It was like a big drawing, a map of womanhood. For the first time in my life, I realized I was also on the map: 'Well then, I'm normal.'

Suddenly it all made perfect sense. I was at the male end of female. There were bits of me I'd hidden away that now I could be OK about. Shortly afterwards, I was with two other ladies doing the catering for a womanhood workshop, and we started laughing, discussing how each of us would do it differently. That weekend was such fun, seeing our differences and celebrating our uniqueness instead of all trying to be the same.

Shortly after Martin and I were married, a fuse blew on something in the house and I went to change it. But I then thought to myself that I shouldn't, because that was the man's job. I had this fixed idea of the manly role and the lady's role. But after the workshop I began to see that these were the things I did, and that was OK, because my husband and I both had weaknesses and could cover for each other.

Even though I'm at the male end of the continuum, I'm still a woman. But there are other things I enjoy that a man might enjoy. Realizing that, I became able to relax more in who I was and begin exploring the bits of me I had hidden.

I had wanted to join the Air Force as a mechanic when I left school. They said, 'Does she understand she's stepping into a man's world?' All I had been taught was that I should get married and have kids. 'You don't need a career, because you're not going to stick around long enough to have one.' I could have done a whole range of things, but never did. I've made peace with that now, and I've already begun to see it redeemed. The opportunities are just beginning to open up for me. I now accept that I can become the person God created me to be, which I never realized before.

When I began praying about this, I was unable to pray, 'God, help me to become the woman you created me to be,' because I had a stereotype of a particular woman in my mind, and I thought that if I became the woman God created me to be I'd end up just like her. And I didn't want that. So instead I prayed, 'God, help me to become the *person* you created me to be.' I've still got some way to go, but I am happy knowing I'm going to become who I was intended to be before all the damage happened.

Susan once talked at a Ladies' Night about becoming unique. I didn't see how it could ever be something I wanted, or could enjoy, because of the damage I'd experienced as a child. Deal is a very white community, and at the time we were one of the few dark-skinned families in the town. So we were picked on and abused quite badly, which also contributed to how I felt about myself.

As I grew up, I hid bits of myself more and more, but you can't hide your colour very easily. So I would walk around apologizing for who I was. After Susan's talk about becoming more unique, I was devastated. I went home and burst into tears, because I wanted to be white, to fit in and hide in the crowd. But when there's a crowd of white faces I stick out like a sore thumb. And my abilities, interests and gifting also made me stick out like a sore thumb. Yet when I met the person God created me to be, I realized she was acceptable just as she was. I didn't even notice she was a woman; she was just a person who was alive and bright and who loved being herself. That helped me to see that the self-hate I carried was actually wrong, because she liked herself!

I had to separate out these two people, one who was the person God had created me to be, whom I called Nicola Kate, and the other person whom I had created and hated with a passion. I just wanted to wipe her off the face of the earth. Later, I was having a session with Susan when she said, 'You can take either one of you out of here today, and leave the other one behind.' It was a moment of decision: a horrible one or a wonderful one. 'I want to be Nicola Kate,' I said.

There was a meeting that evening and I was asked to answer the door. As people arrived, they were shocked. They told me I looked different. I felt different inside but hadn't realized that it showed. Someone said, 'We saw you today in town, but we didn't see *you*, did we?' And I just grinned and said, 'No, you didn't.' I had changed sides. I decided I would now try to be the person God had created me to be, rather than hate the horrible person I had become.

We all draw much of our womanhood from our fathers. But my father died, and my stepfather showed a lot of anger towards us. Some of his anger was towards my mother, but he took it out on me. I assumed it was all my fault, but now I'm beginning to realize it wasn't. I still think I'm going to do something wrong and I don't have any confidence in myself at all, except now and again on a workshop when I know I am becoming the person that God created me to be. I know there are areas of my womanhood I haven't ventured into yet, that will appear as I get rid of the damage done to me by others.

So as my children grow and develop, I know I've got to teach Michael that it's OK for him to be a man and Martin will teach Deborah that it's OK for her to be a woman. I've watched Deborah blossom in ways that I never did, because Martin encourages her. We're both still learning with our children. But that's another whole part of womanhood.

I used to beat myself up all the time with what I'd done to my children. Now I accept that I did make some mistakes, but God has been redeeming them. It's made such a difference to know that the children are perfectly able to let the harm go, really quickly. God can redeem for them the damage that I have done to them.

When we first came to Christ Church, Michael showed many of the symptoms of being borderline autistic, so one of the few safe places for him was in his own little world, and he couldn't come out because there was this angry woman waiting to harm him if he did.[2] But after I'd met who God created me to be, about a year or so later, I met Michael for the first time – he was 6 or 7 by then. It was quite shocking. Martin and I had done some homework and suddenly this real little boy popped out.[3] A curly-haired, grinning little boy that we'd never seen before. It became safe for him to come out, because of the way I'd changed.

One of the big things I fought and struggled with for a long time was that the woman has to start doing homework first.[4] But I have learnt that if the woman creates a safe space, everybody's true selves can begin to appear. For instance, if the woman decides to love her man, she can make the relationship a safe place for him. Peace is then possible.

For a long time Susan and Peter were telling us both that somebody had to stop the war, and I kept saying, 'Well, he can do it,' and Martin was saying, 'Well, she can do it.' Then one day I realized it isn't important who's right. It's about who's at peace. Anybody at any time, in any marriage, has a choice to say, 'I'm sorry, I'm wrong,' or, 'I'm sorry, I don't want to do this any more,' or, 'Let's just stop.' We started doing this, and we went from a place where we were sometimes even fighting each other physically to not fighting at all. I now see that what really matters is our willingness to see that it doesn't matter who's right and who's wrong. The important thing is whether you're willing to live differently, willing to walk away from 'That's not my fault . . .'

What I hadn't realized was that you learn almost everything you know about marriage from your parents. We both came into the marriage with a lot of baggage. We both hated men and women, and we beat each other up with it. He hated me, I hated him, and we just lived that way until we realized that it wasn't a good way to live. So along the road of discovering my womanhood I also discovered what manhood was. For both of us it's about becoming the people God created us to be. And we realized we could choose to work together.

I've got weaknesses that are Martin's strengths, and he's got weaknesses that are my strengths. Hence I'm doing all the bookkeeping and paperwork for his business. He's good at multi-tasking, and very good at providing and giving us a roof over our heads. He can put pictures on the wall: I can't – they'd just fall down again. But if a light switch breaks, I know how to repair it. We've started to realize that we can choose, even work together, and complement each other.

If we leave the baggage of our pasts behind and start again, we can choose how our marriage grows. So for our twentieth wedding anniversary he bought me a new wedding ring as a declaration that we wanted to start again, have a new marriage. The first twenty years we were learning, and now we are no longer going to throw our toxic history at each other.

I have also learnt that most men don't really understand how to love, and that if they are willing, women can teach them. Again, the woman has to go first. I can decide to love him anyway, and honour and respect him. That helps him to grow as a person, and then it flows out of him, back to me. But if I put hate, bitterness and anger into him, that's what I get back. It is the woman who is most able to break the cycle.

It's as if there's a big pot of goodness that every family has. If everybody is taking out of the pot all the time, very soon it becomes empty and there's nothing left. But if you keep putting something in, even though it may take a while, eventually other people in the family notice, and they also begin putting something in. Then there's enough for anybody to come and take out of the pot what and when they need to.

One day I realized I didn't have to try to be a better woman. I can't be a better Nicola Kate; I've just got to learn to relax and be her. I can never prove I'm a woman. I already am, and always will be. I can welcome it and work with it, or I can fight it, which for a long time I did. Now I've realized that women have the biggest opportunity to change the world around them, in a way that men don't. There's a gift of giving life that women carry.

Welcoming womanhood is about becoming the unique person that God created each one of us to be. There's no other person on the face of the earth who can be a better Nicola Kate than I am. God's put it all in there, and it's how willing I am to look at the damage in me that determines how far I'll get at becoming her. I do want to become her. At the beginning of my journey I was determined to 'sort Martin out', because I thought that was the way to save our marriage. But now I am willing to be 'sorted' myself, because then I can offer that hope to other people while enjoying it myself.

I am learning how to be an oasis in a desert, in a way that everything you touch you can give life to, and continue to give life to, on and on. Women carry this in a way men don't. It's a gift I don't really understand. I can't even put it into words: it's a special life-giving gift that women have. And it can change families and communities, because even in today's society, where people are breaking up, a woman can still influence the children, the husbands, the fathers, the grandparents. And you can affect the wider circle of people around you in a way that men don't. So although I've still got a lot to learn about womanhood, I think I'm starting to find it quite exciting.

A Journey of Hope, Discovery and Life
Norma Davidson

I'm 62, married to Bob, and we live in Portland, Oregon. Bob has two children from his previous marriage. We now have two grandchildren. We are both retired. I've been part of Valley View Evangelical Church for thirty-three years – the church where Derry has been the pastor for the last few years.

Hope

From my mom and her mom I learnt very early to care more about others than for myself. By the age of 9 I was getting pretty good at it, so my mother sent me for two weeks to stay with my paternal grandmother. She was alone and suffering from Alzheimer's. I remember sleeping with the bed against the wall and lying in front of her, so that if she got out it would wake me. I could follow her, and would eventually get her back into bed. Those two weeks were scary, lonely. So I learnt early to live in other people's worlds and meet their needs and expectations, and didn't really learn to value who I was.

As I grew into adulthood, care-giving became my identity. In the process I lost 'me'. Life rolled by and I easily slipped into my stride as a caregiver. I was a schoolteacher caring for children. Then I'd come home to family members needing my special care. There was never time to think about me, or what I might want. Besides, it seemed selfish to think about me.

For ten years after my retirement I cared for my own mom, and also for my husband during serious illnesses. I devoted myself to living their lives. I waited on them, catered to their needs. As they both began returning to better health, I didn't realize that the lost me was just about dead and buried.

The lost me, combined with emotional and physical exhaustion, brought such devastation that I began breaking down physically and emotionally. I woke up one morning with my whole body jerking and twitching, and over the weeks got to the place where I couldn't even walk. I couldn't get food to my mouth with cutlery, so I ate with my fingers. I had trouble breathing. After lots of tests, the doctors sent me to the mental health clinic. I felt as though there was no hope for my condition, and now nothing to hope for in my future.

Although I had been a lifelong Christian, my faith was no longer sustaining me. I was a broken and shaken woman, at a place where I decided God cared about everyone else but me. I felt that he had abandoned me.

Through my pastor, the Lord brought Peter and Susan halfway round the world into my very own living room. They brought me a message from God's heart, of hope and reassurance that there was another me – not just the me I had known. They talked about my having a true me within my spirit, who possessed value in and for herself.[5] It struck me how valuable I must be to God for Him to transport two people from England to bring me this message of a new and vibrant life. I still find myself being amazed by that.

They spent time with me talking about how much God loved me, and how He desired an intimate daily relationship with me. They also said that our spiritual lives greatly impact both our physical lives and our health.[6] I had hope, for the first time I could remember, that God wanted me to live a new life with Him in this world. I didn't have to just sit there in my pain and sickness, waiting for the promise of heaven, to find healing. In this miraculous way the Lord gave me a message of real life, and began restoring the real person He had created me to be. I made up my mind that very day that I was going to put my hand in His and allow Him to lead me to the abundant life that was promised me in Scripture. That day I felt like I jumped off a cliff holding His hand.

As I began this journey, I listened to Susan's tapes and read the Bible notes explaining spiritual concepts, teachings and tools. They really helped me, since I was doing the journey alone for six months before I attended my first workshop. On one of the tapes was a meditation in which we imagined a well we could go to for refreshment.[7] My well was nothing more than an old blue handpump in the middle of a dusty yard. I had to pump my own water, and water only flowed when I pumped. Over time I asked the Lord to replace my desolate well. He took me to a hot spring I had frequented as a child. The hot and cold water flowed together into a creek and over a waterfall into a small swimming pool. He invited me to swim with Him. I was struggling with difficult issues and when I tired, He would call me to the pool to play. I found that I could meet Him there whenever I chose to. We would splash and laugh together in the pool, then we would sit on the sand and talk. There I found rest, peace, love and hope.

During that first year, the Lord reacquainted me with my true self. I lost the jerking, and my body began to be restored and healed. The healing occurred slowly over a couple of years, as my spirit was restored. Today I walk normally, I breathe normally, and I eat too much with a properly held fork!

This journey with the Lord has truly been an enlightening, life-changing discovery of who I am, seen through His eyes. At one point I recalled that my mom's parents had kept a large land turtle chained to the clothesline that stood between our two houses. During the day the turtle would crawl around in the rocky dust and grass that grew under the clothesline. As a young girl I frequently watched the turtle through the bedroom window, and felt sad about his dismal life.

As I began my *Rapha* journey, the Lord would periodically bring this picture back to my mind. I would ask Him what He was trying to show me, but the picture would be placed in the background as I worked through another issue that seemed more pressing at the time. Nothing triggered anything more, so I waited.

I attended a womanhood workshop with the ladies in my *Rapha* group. The workshop left me irritated but smug. I thought it didn't apply to me. On the *Gender Continuum* I scored halfway over into the middle of the male side. It had pinned me where I figured I might be. I had a visual orientation, and didn't multi-task very well, but I already knew that. After all, I'd been living with me for a long time.

Throughout the workshop the picture of the turtle kept returning and continued to puzzle me. I asked the Lord about it again and He simply told me to wait. I asked Susan about the picture and she said the Lord would show me its meaning when He was ready.[8] So I waited, working on other homework as the Lord directed me. He led me through issues of slavery and living in isolation.

I attend a *Rapha* support group with other women who accept, love and stand with me.[9] I've never had many women friends, so have come to value their friendship highly. A year or so after the workshop they wanted to listen to the tapes from the womanhood workshop again. I reluctantly agreed to go back there. At the same time the Lord asked me to start using my left hand. (I was right-handed, so it was a strange thing to ask.) I did so for a couple of months, until the prompting faded. I think the Lord was trying to move me out of being stuck in an intellectual realm, into my more feminine side. It worked!

I meet regularly with two other ladies and we call ourselves a troika.[10] This has encouraged and helped me to work through delicate feminine issues that I carried. It was in this group that I discovered that the Lord had given me the name of 'Princess among the stars'. Here I had the time and space to take a good look at my self-image.

While I was listening a second time to the womanhood workshop tapes, the picture of the turtle returned, and this time I could not get it out of my head. As I studied the turtle, I found that it hides inside its shell for protection. I told the Lord I would trust Him and not fear what He wanted to show me. He led me to the story of Samson, showing me that Samson was strong, cunning and courageous, but vulnerable because no one watched his back.

My mentor gave me a word from the Lord: it was 'courage'. Little did I know how much I needed courage to do what was ahead of me. It came to me that I was the turtle. And in the days ahead God showed me how I had hidden inside the shell for protection. He revealed to me that since I could not embrace womanhood, I had instead chosen an intellectual life without gender. I had become a student and eventually a teacher, living a life of strict, rigid control, completely denying my womanhood. I hadn't worn a dress for years, so I purchased some as the Lord directed, but they were all denim and not very feminine.

As the days passed, the Lord showed and taught me many things. One time, He showed me lots of angels guarding my back, with me sitting in front of a great shining light. I told the Lord I wanted Him to be my protection. There, as I faced the light, He took me back to the day when as a child, sitting under the clothesline, with the turtle in my lap, I had declared I did not want to become a woman. And since I couldn't be a man I would be neither – a non-gender person. I would build a wall of protection around myself, just like the turtle.

I even remembered going to the doctor with severe headaches, an ongoing condition since childhood. He told me I had turtle syndrome! With stress I tightened my shoulders and pulled my head down. It created pain in my shoulders, neck and head. I spent lots of time in physical therapy, trying to get relief from the chronic pain. I began to see the Lord had been trying to tell me about this for a long time. I wasn't ready to hear and see until I came to this point in my walk with Him.

Facing the light, with the angels behind me, I repeated that the Lord was my protection and systematically, strip by strip, I removed the back of the shell. With a bloody back I walked into the light and felt it fold around me and hold me. A part of me was healed and restored that day.

So the weekly listening to the womanhood workshop tapes continued. I thought it was a waste of my precious time: after all, I didn't have any womanhood issues. Not me! Over the next few weeks the Lord reminded me of how I had been working through womanhood issues in my homework, facing what my early childhood experiences had taught me. I had worked through one lie after another. I believed that being a woman was unsafe; it meant pain, aversion, shame, embarrassment, isolation, secrecy and being a nonentity.

He showed me how many of my issues with

womanhood were based on these lies. For instance, I chose to believe that women were unsafe, so I feared being with them. Fearing women, and women's friendship, and living as a non-gender entity formed the basis of all my life's decisions, together with the loss of my femininity. I regularly said to the Lord, 'Please forgive me for being a woman.' So over the years the shell of protection around me grew even thicker. The Lord had been preparing me to find out the meaning of the picture of the turtle all along, but I didn't realize it.

On my journey ever since, I have been dismantling the consequences of the choices to be a non-gender person. The turtle life gave me protection. Now God was asking me to live in vulnerability. That has been difficult and required lots of courage. I thought I had learnt a lot from the turtle, but it was only the beginning. A few weeks later I was told I had breast cancer.

Wrestling through those first days of knowing was agonizing. Day by day I listed before the Lord my hopes and dreams, giving each one to Him. I knew that the new life I now possessed might never get a chance to blossom. I wondered why the Lord had brought me all this new life. So that He could just take it away again? But as I continued to sit in His presence and let Him talk to me, I came to the conclusion that He was worth it all. If I never lived another day, this new relationship with Him was enough.

My decisions had brought me countless physical sufferings with female-related health issues, and breast cancer was now the latest part of that. I found it very difficult to forgive myself for losing the things in life that by carrying this baggage I had lost. After surgery, when I lost one of my breasts, I became filled with grief and 'sorries' for all the damage I had done to myself and for all the years I had wasted. I could not get beyond it.

Listening to one of the tapes, where Susan talks about sitting in the river of our own stinking garbage, I knew I was sitting in my own smelly river. I asked the Lord how to get out of that river, into His river of grace and mercy. He told me I needed to take His hand, walk out with Him and be washed. He then washed me with the soap of forgiveness. Only the sadness and grief remained. I needed self-forgiveness. So I crawled out of the river, took another bar of the soap of forgiveness and washed myself. I kept repeating to myself, 'I forgive you, I forgive you.' This time I was able to go with open arms into the river of grace and mercy.

The water was so clear and effervescent. It tingled and bubbled on my skin and in my heart. I was truly forgiven! My Friend gave me a bar of beautiful red soap with a river of pink flowing through it. I had been forgiven and washed in the blood of Jesus. Through His blood I had also been able to forgive myself. Now I'm finding, at the end of each day, after I have made a blunder, I can look at that bar of soap and feel again the effervescent water of the river of mercy and grace.

As I have walked through the cancer struggles, I have found God beginning to restore my gender and my femininity. I listen to Him as He leads me into becoming a real woman. Right now I'm not sure what that looks like, but that's OK because He knows.

As I've written this story, I have become aware that the Lord also prepared me. During the fall and winter months just before my cancer discovery, the story of David dancing before the Lord created a deep longing within my heart. I longed to dance before Him. Well, as 'Princess among the stars' I began to dream of dancing before Him under the stars. One cold, icy night, deep in the middle of winter, I dressed warmly and put on all my sparkly necklaces. I put on long fancy earrings and a tiara, and stepped out into the starry night.

I was transformed from a short, dumpy old woman into a beautiful princess dancing before the Lord. During the days of fear, dealing with cancer, and even now, when I close my eyes, I slip back into that moment. God is so big and so close, He lifts me up in His hands. I look into His eyes and we dance . . . and dance . . . and dance . . . together.

Some Comments

Both Nicola and Norma are on a journey of becoming the women they were created to be. It brings huge amounts of hope to discover that the person God first created is not entirely lost, but temporarily buried under layers of historic damage, toxic emotion and lies that we believe to be true. The same is also true of men, although in a slightly different way, as we will see in the following chapter.

This 'true self' is unique, and over time, through the authenticity of our journey with the Lord, we begin to discover we can live at peace with our growing uniqueness, as we become more like Christ. Many of us have made the same mistake as Nicola and Norma, judging and condemning ourselves whenever we fail to live up to the masks and the stereotype we believe we should be, or which others require or expect us to be. All of this falseness, Christian or otherwise, needs to be taken away by the Lord, with our close co-operation.

The idea of loving ourselves is a strange one to many of us. So is the idea that God wants to bring us such healing that we develop the capacity to love ourselves. But the Lord already knows that most of us do not willingly love ourselves. However, until we have made peace with who we really are physically, emotionally and spiritually, we will know little of the capacity to love others or Him. All of us have parts or aspects of ourselves that we do not like, so we all need to make some progress in this area. We are not speaking here of indulgent self-love, or narcissism, but the type of righteous self-love that allows all of us to honour ourselves and others.

Nicola makes several mentions of the positive impact her journey had on her marriage. We adopt the view that it is rarely what happens to us in our marriage, but rather the baggage we bring into our marriage, that ultimately sinks us. Most of what happens to us after we are married merely reflects the baggage collected and learnt long before. It is often easy to predict what will go wrong in a marriage, on the basis of the unfinished homework the person carries into the marriage. We therefore treat people as individuals, from the homework and baggage perspective, so that by doing their journey in their marriage, over time, they begin to positively change. They naturally begin to become the person their partner needs them to be, rather than spending all their time blaming or seeking to change their partner. The greatest gift one can bring to one's marriage is a right relationship with Christ, oneself and others. This comes about by a wholeness journey.

Here in CCD and *Rapha* we are a community celebrating uniqueness and diversity, rather than conformity and control. This is unusual, since many churches would expect people to conform – personally, relationally and Biblically. There is a culture within parts of the church that unconsciously says, 'We are mature Christians, so to be Christlike you need to be like us.' Here, we turn this attitude upside down, by suggesting that all of us are unique, will hear the Lord in different ways and sort out the baggage that is unique to us, and in becoming Christlike will actually somehow become more unique.

You have read this happening as Nicola became more like Nicola Kate, and Norma became more like Norma. This makes life very interesting in our community and on the *Rapha* journey. We all start in different places, ending with maturity in Christ, but will be different to the person we were because of all the Lord has said to us, and all we have done to change.

Notes

[1] This concept of sin against ourselves is a fundamental one in our work. We have all made decisions that while appearing wise at the time, later prove to have harmed us. Scripture is full of examples of men and women who did harm to themselves, e.g. Moses, Saul, David, Peter, etc.

[2] Nicola is referring here to the strength of feeling she carried against men. She had been hurt by men so much as a child that she'd buried the hate and anger she carried towards them but was unwittingly expressing it in an emotional way by laying it on her son.

[3] Such moments are a common consequence of homework: when a parent lets go of a significant area of damage in their life, the child will frequently spontaneously do the same. It especially applies to children under the age of 10.

[4] In the early days of our work, we usually encouraged the woman to start her journey first, as she often had more complex layers of damage to work through.

[5] One of the ways that we help people to grow in their wholeness and relationship with God is to show them that as they look at themselves from God's perspective, they can begin to see who He created them to be, their 'true self'. In time all this damage can leave them, and it is as though it had never happened.

[6] This simple principle undergirds much of our work. We see many examples of physical healing and restoration after someone has been able to let go of significant emotional and

spiritual damage. But we do not claim to have a physical healing ministry; wholeness overflows into all the parts of our personhood.

7 Meditation on Scripture and its themes is an ancient tradition in the church. We frequently use meditation to help people focus on meeting and hearing from the Lord. Some find this more helpful than others.

8 We follow this simple principle when the Lord begins speaking to someone. Rather than providing an interpretation ourselves, we will always encourage the person to keep listening to Him and let Him tell them when He and they are ready. It builds greater trust in God and avoids dependence on anyone else.

9 There are a number of *Rapha* support/discipleship groups that have begun to form once we have done workshops in an area.

10 A troika is a carriage pulled in parallel by three horses. We began troikas among men in Deal several years ago, but they have spread to women's groups as well. A group of three can be a good balance for either men or women.

4

Manhood

Nicola and Norma have introduced us to womanhood. But one aspect of our community life that has really surprised us is what we have been learning together about manhood.

Many of us have grown up with the assumption that man is a solitary being, independent, self-assured, strong, showing little or no emotion. In fact, our western culture adores this image of the rugged, self-reliant male. He saves the world! Even in the church, we keep reading about the solitary saint, the spiritual hero working alone with his God. But here in the community, men together have discovered the opposite. Martin's story illustrates some of the significance of discovering healthy life-giving relationships among men. Growing up in a female environment, he had learnt about men from women and wrongly taken up some of these values. Liam's story is very different. He had become a 'nice' Christian man, and hidden the depth of his manhood, which was wrapped up in his pain. He had to find and engage all of this before he was able to begin to see his manhood.

Both men you are about to meet are successful

professionals, who have many years of relationship with God. They were both shocked to discover that from God's perspective, even after many years of Christianity they were still so much less than the men they were created to be.

This Man Martin
Martin Carnall

I'm 47 and married to Nicola, whom you have already met. I was born in Essex but have lived in Deal since 1970. I joined the church in the early eighties, moving quickly into leadership. I've recently started my own business, surprisingly successful, offering management consultancy and training, and support services to colleges and industry. I enjoy playing with my kids, cooking and music.

I suppose I thought I was OK as a man. Most others would have said so too. But in hindsight I can see that the model of maleness, and its programming, were inherently flawed. The result was a man who wasn't at all the way he should have been.

My parents separated quite violently when I was about 5. So I remember lying in my bed when I was about 3 or 4, when the lights went out, hearing them row, feeling as a little boy that I was inconvenient.

My father left and my mother and I went wandering among her family, all over the country. She had a lot of sisters, so I was in a world of aunties. There were uncles as well, but I only saw them in the morning, before they went to work, and in the evening. The world was a world of women.

Then my father won custody of me, but somehow in that process I had to make the decision to live with my mother or with my father. I was 6 or 7 years of age, and I had already learnt that, as a male, every single decision you make will cost you. You win this, but you lose that. In my personal life, I became somebody who would never make decisions. I pleased my father by choosing to live with him, and I lost my mother. If I'd chosen to live with my mother, I would have lost my father.

When I came down to Kent, I was introduced to my father's business partner and his wife. I didn't enjoy living with my father or my new 'aunt and uncle'. So not only did the decision I'd made cost me my mother, but I didn't get to spend much time with my father either. Instead, I had this other pair of parents, and that was incredibly disappointing. They were disappointed in me too. I wasn't the little boy that they wanted; I was some other inconvenient little boy.

My uncle and father were ruled by this woman. She managed the business, she engineered meetings, she manipulated, she controlled, she used all of her womanly, canny business sense and her female intuition. The men just worked. I got the impression men were bred to work, and that's what I was being groomed for. This lady needed three men around her and I decided I wasn't going to be one of them.

They arranged for me to go to prep school, as a condition of my coming to live with my father, and I then went on to public school (all within the private, fee-paying/scholarship sector). Coming from a council estate on the outskirts of London to a public school in south-east Kent, I stood out like a sore thumb. So public school started as a bit of a disappointment too.

I was growing up with all sorts of conflicting models and a huge amount of pain and disappointment. And that turned me into quite a bitter, angry person. When I reached my teens I was incredibly rebellious, continuing the pattern of disappointment. Can you imagine that bright, intelligent council estate kid given the opportunity of public school? Small classes, graduate teachers, lots of resources, sport every day. I should have thrived, but I just blended in with the middle.

I certainly didn't want to fail, because then you're the odd one out, but I didn't want to excel, for the same reason. I was living out my anger by giving everybody a really good lesson in what disappointment is. And the pain and disappointment of my childhood were just growing in intensity all the time. I very much disliked my life, and could pretty much predict that tomorrow was going to be disappointing. Which, of course, it was.

After a short, defiant spell as an apprentice journalist on the local paper, I went back into the family business. I became one of the worker bees after all, the three men serving the household ruled by the woman, and still being reminded that I could have been an army officer. So I went out and joined the Territorial Army as a private soldier, while working in the construction industry, ostensibly being trained in how to manage the family's building business but being most content digging drains. Disappointment again, fuelling further anger. I eventually got to the stage where I really hated my life and then went into self-destruct mode. I went on a drinking binge that lasted maybe four-and-a-half-years. And I later discovered that I hated myself for what I'd done, for wasting my life and my opportunities.

I despised my father and my uncle. They were rough-tough men, but served the woman. They were just on this planet to work and die. So I was incredibly angry at God for allowing this to continue. Men were only created to work, slog their guts out and then die. There was no possible benefit to being male. I didn't like being male.

School had taught me one model of being male, and

my family life had taught me another. Combine the two,
and you have a very angry and very disappointed young
man who hates life and himself, hates women with a
vengeance, and really doesn't think very much of men at
all.

Then I met Christ and my life completely changed.
Although I didn't find any men that I really admired and
wanted to be like in the church, I was thoroughly
welcomed and became fully part of it. I became part of
the leadership, became a 'man' in the church, while I was
actually still a very angry, disappointed, bitter man who
had, from my perspective, a very sad life. I brought all
this into the church. I guess I owe the church a huge
apology.

In addition, over a period of about fifteen years I lost
my relationship with Christ. I no longer knew Him
because I'd buried myself in knowing *about* Him.

I started my journey on the basis that my marriage was
falling apart and so was my faith.

My position in relation to those two things got fixed,
but that was only part of it. The journey is about learning
God's perspective and owning what you then see, taking
responsibility for it, looking at the root issues, saying
sorry, removing the wrong patterns and living another
way.

In doing the journey I had to look at a whole series of
issues, including what had been done to me by both of
my parents as well as by my so-called aunt and uncle. But
more importantly, I had to look at what I had done with
that, and what I had done to myself.[1] I began to see that
my anger and my hatred of people had made me
manipulative and controlling. What I had done was learn
how to survive in a world where woman is the cleverer.

So I had learnt how to read her and think what she was
thinking and to know what she wanted. I would read

body language; I would read minds. I lived in fear of getting the blame, of being found out, of it all going wrong. I'd learnt to be what she needed me to be and I despised myself for that. But I discovered on the journey that men and women are entirely different beings and they function in entirely different ways. Once I became aware of that, I could see more clearly what I had done to myself, and what had been done to me.

The hardest thing for me in all of this was to engage my emotions – to live this, to feel it, to actually let it possess me, my anger, my pain, my disappointment, to actually allow my emotions out. Big boys don't cry. I would rationalize everything rather than feel it. When I finally got to the place where I could actually say sorry to me, which was quite a long time into the journey, I was also able to say I should never have been a soldier or a builder. It's not who I am and I had to make peace with that. I had modelled myself around what people needed me to be. That isn't actually who the man Martin should have been.

So my hope grows as I start to let go of the pain.

Moving into the journey gives you a chance to see these things. To engage them, to relive that feeling and that emotion and then to say sorry to yourself, to others, to God, for you, for others. And to invite the Holy Spirit to redeem the situation. You start possibly with the anger, then the pain and then the drives that locked it all in place: this curse, that declaration. That's where you actually meet Christ.

In finding this man, I needed other men. I distrusted men entirely, though, so I had to learn to do the journey with other men. The journey requires relationships because you have to go into emotion. You learn to trust again because you have to. So, in going on this journey, I was beginning to realize what relationships with men

Changed Lives

really were. And through that I was discovering what manhood actually is, with other men who were learning it with me.

I discovered that to get into that place for me was quite violent. I would cough and I would spit, and blood vessels would burst in my eyes, and I would be sick. I learnt that you couldn't do this on your own. At some of our men's meetings we used to end up with a bowl each and a roll of kitchen towel!

The hope grows that you can change. History doesn't have to repeat itself. And when situations come round as they have in the past, you will respond very differently, because you're actually very different. You aren't that person any more and you're seeing a different perspective.

Your relationship with Christ is growing; you're seeing Him, you're meeting Him and you're hearing His voice. And when you're on your hands and knees sobbing your heart out, saying sorry to yourself, saying sorry to the people involved in what you're reaching into, you actually find your hands are wrapped around Christ's feet and you are on your knees in front of Him. One of the most profound things that can happen in any of the troikas or men's groups is when you're deep into emotionally engaging something and a voice from a man alongside you says very, very gently, 'And where is Jesus? What's He doing?' Almost invariably He's crying or He's saying sorry.[2] You also discover in this process that that's what being a man is: allowing yourself to be broken and vulnerable.[3]

But I wasn't going to allow myself to be vulnerable. I was vulnerable as a kid, and look how I was hurt. Instead I will keep distant from myself, my true self and who I really am. I will keep distant from my relationships, so they're going to be disappointing and they're going to fall apart. And I will keep myself distant from God, so my relationship with Him is going to be nondescript and disappointing.

The next thing I had to learn to let go of was my fear. In letting go of my fear, I started to dare to tell God what sort of a man I actually wanted to be. I started to give myself permission to begin thinking about the future. You can't tell God the sort of man you want to be without talking about what the future could be.

And when you put together a group of men, daring to talk about that together, you suddenly discover that manhood is actually nothing like what we had programmed ourselves to believe it was.

Jesus, for some reason, chooses to deal with men in public. So for me to tell God the sort of man I wanted to be meant that I had to be around men, but not in the way I had experienced in the building industry or military. To be able to cry in front of men, to be vulnerable, to allow another man to hug me and protect me and weep in front of Christ on my behalf or dare to agree with me before God that what I dreamed should happen and say, 'Yeah, let that be!' Other men knowing your secret thoughts.

Manhood in God is about passion, tenderness and gentleness, and standing back to back.

There is a passionate and right relationship among men that comes out of the relationship that the man has with himself and with Christ. But you can't have that relationship with Christ unless you have it with yourself. You can't have it with yourself unless you're prepared to have it with others. So there's a triangle of relationship.

We need to spiritually father one another, be brothers for one another and be sons for one another. So, welcoming my manhood, I have had to learn to be a son again, and to be a father and a brother, as well as a husband and a friend.

Taking responsibility for the person I had become was the starting point in welcoming my manhood. This is the person that I am and it's well short of the man that I want to be or could be.

Now I'm on a journey of becoming the man I could be. I've had to learn not to judge, to choose not to judge, to lay down my hatred, my anger and my bitterness. In doing that, I'm finding a gentleness, a compassion and a brokenness, and finding out how to be broken. It's not easy, letting God break you and letting others, by what they feel, touch you and break you. But if my tears are never far away and I'm able to be sorry on behalf of someone, for someone, or just generally to God, for the situation or for me, and let that break me, then I know I'm not far from being the man that I really am.

Brokenness removes the male posturing, arrogance and dominance. So the man you get is clearly visible, and therefore his gifting, his anointing and his calling in Christ are also clearly visible. They are not owned by him, but rest neatly on him.

Now I've dared to say to God that I want to be a certain man. And the immediate response when you make such a declaration is that whatever stands between you and having that, becoming that man, should show itself.

About the time I first made peace with the fact that I should never have been a soldier or a builder, I was picking up a door – just a lightweight, hollow-core door – and a muscle tore in my right arm. All of a sudden my big, strong right arm was taken away.[4] I'm not the builder or the soldier any more; that's not where my strength as a man lies. So if I am to be strong at all, where does my strength lie?

Even more dramatic was the way I discovered that I actually didn't welcome life. 'I don't want to be alive if life is this disappointing.' I was involved in a multiple car pile-up that closed the motorway. The car looked like a concertina. The fire brigade were amazed that I just opened the door and got out. And when the policeman taking down the details asked for my date of birth, he said, 'What are you doing, driving on your birthday?'

I remember heading for the pile-up of traffic; the cars in front were all braking hard and I knew I was going to pile into them. I just closed my eyes and for the first time I said to God, 'I'm sorry.' And I knew for the first time in forty-plus years that I actually wanted to be alive. Life wasn't disappointing any more: it had hope; it had a future. I was saying sorry that I'd exposed myself to a situation where it was now all coming to an end. Instead, I was able to walk away from that experience, thanks to God. It was a miracle. But I realized then that there was an awful lot that had a right to kill me, because of the way I'd lived and all the self-cursing declarations I'd made. You couldn't find a greater illustration than being in a near-fatal accident on your birthday! There were 364 other days that it could have happened – why on your birthday?

I had to welcome life before I could welcome my manhood: I want to have a future, I want to have a life, I don't want to live with disappointment any more but want to live with success, in God's terms of what success is. That was the turning point.

I knew that I carried huge amounts of judgement, bitterness, anger and hate. But by choosing to live, I was now in a position where I chose to see all that would keep me from living as I should. You've got to want to live at peace with yourself, with who you are and who you're becoming, and also at peace with who you've been.

So I'm not a man who has a strong right arm. I'm a man who wants to live, which means not only do I want life, but also I want to give life and to be where life is given, to encourage it and to promote it. That's manhood.

But I became aware that I was so frightened that history would repeat itself or that I would fail or disappoint, that I tried to model the person I wanted to become on those people I admired and trusted and knew weren't failing, instead of becoming 'me'. So God couldn't actually let me flourish.

I was controlling, because of fear. I was petrified that someone would step into my new, fresh, wonderful, unlimited world and say, 'You're a fake, you're a fraud. You used to be an alcoholic, you're just a builder.'

Recently God took me to a place where I could see there was a choice: Do I want to accept that I've got as far as I can in my journey? After all, where I am would still be good: I could live very well and prosper and have a huge amount of peace in my life. Or do I actually want to go further?

If I'm to go on, all vestiges of the old Martin have to go. I've never been at this place before. I can't do the rest of this journey measuring my progress against the man I was before, because the two don't equate. Only a broken, vulnerable man can become this new Martin. So I'm at the edge of the world I know and understand, and I'm at the end of myself.

In ancient times they had the idea that the earth was flat, and at the edge of the world the oceans just fell off. So if they went to the edge of the world they'd fall off as well. I saw myself standing on a rock at the edge of the world. There's a mist rising as the oceans are pouring over the edge, and beyond the mist is a pale blue nothingness where God lives. So in any direction, apart from forwards, the nearest land mass is thousands of miles away. I've got my arms out, trying to keep my balance, and I can see myself teetering, ready to go over the edge. Then God comes from behind me and makes eye contact with me, saying, 'Well, go on then,' and carries on past. He doesn't even stop to talk. As He's going past, I say, 'But what if I fall?' and as He's disappearing off into His realm, He's saying over his shoulder, 'But what if you fly?'

For me, the next step towards becoming the man that I am is to learn to live in freefall. So I'm choosing just to be in freefall, so that I can fly. Not choosing any particular direction to fly in or any particular style or technique to fly with, I just fall and let God provide the lift.

A Journey Into Change
Liam McCann

I'm 42, was born in Belfast and now live in Bristol. I'm married to Dawn, with three children: David (12), Ashling (11) and Joseph (9). I was born into a Roman Catholic family but am now part of an Anglican church.

For a long time I have thought of myself as an OK bloke, nice enough, friendly, helpful. I have called myself a Christian for about twenty years, have gone to church and done lots of the usual church things. But the question that has really bugged me is why am I not able to be like other people in church, who seem so straightforward and uncomplicated. Why have I so little enthusiasm for much of what goes on there? I also find myself thinking about what to do with all my feelings of despair, bitterness, rage, anger and lust. What do I do about feelings of despising myself and others? Also, in the middle of all of these feelings, what do I make of this passionate desire for God that I have?

Let me tell you a bit about myself, and how all this came about. To begin, I am a 42-year-old Irish man. I moved to England in 1990 to get married. I work as a social worker for people with mental health difficulties. I like to think I have a good imagination. I like science fiction and fantasy. Not in a nerdy way, I assure you: I've never gone to the cinema dressed up as Darth Vader or any of that. After all, I am 42! This genre appeals to me because of the scope for imagination, the ability to get behind our 'normal' view of things. Likewise, I am drawn to what I call the 'crazy' stuff in the Bible. Jesus shining like the sun or walking on water and the visions people had of angels, all that 'crazy' stuff that goes beyond our everyday experience of life. I love all the unique ways in which God speaks to people and, as you will see in my story, there are some ways in which God spoke to me that you do not see so much in the Bible. But there was also a need to get my feet back on the ground, to learn to deal with the everyday stuff.

When I was four years old my mother became pregnant. I was old enough to be aware of the excitement of the new arrival. He was due to be born close to Christmas, so I got him a present. When my little brother was born, I guess I must have been a delighted older brother, already thinking of looking after him. Ten weeks after he was born, I woke up one morning to find him dead.

The shock was devastating for our family. It is still hard for me to remember much about what happened at that time. For me, however, there was a double loss, though I didn't notice this till much later. The impact was so devastating on my father that he effectively left the family. He was still physically present, but was no longer a father. He didn't play with me any more or show interest in me, my brothers or my sisters. On reflection, I can see that my family dealt with this event by not dealing with it. We quickly blocked it out, carrying on 'as normal'. Occasionally there would be the odd reference to my brother's death as we grew up, but nothing else. We forgot about it. It was sorted.

As I look back on how I moved from my position of denial about my life, I can see that several things happened over a period of a few years to make me realize I had something to deal with.

When I was in my late twenties I had a picture from God. The picture, as best I can describe it, was of something like a corridor stuffed solid with dark material. At one end of this corridor was me. There was only the tiniest crack in this dark material that ran the length of the corridor, and at the other end shone God in all His brilliance. In my mind's eye the light of God was living, energizing, full of all beauty and wonder. For ages after this picture I was just buoyed up by the fact that God had spoken to me, and I treasured this image in my heart. Never did it occur to me to ask what all the dark material was.

Later my wife gave me some verses from Psalm 73 on a birthday card. Two verses associated with the passage stood out for me: 'When my heart was grieved and my spirit embittered, I was senseless and ignorant; I was a brute beast before you.'

These words resonated inside me in a way that went far beyond intellect. At the time I could make no sense of why they affected me so much. I didn't intellectually recognize what either 'senseless and ignorant', or 'a brute beast' had to do with me.

God was talking to me, but I was unable to face what He was saying to me. So just as when I and my family decided not to face my brother's death, I didn't face what God wanted to say to me.

During the nineties my wife and I joined a Christian community. We stayed there for about fifteen months. Living in this community was, up to that point, the worst experience of my life. I absolutely hated it, and found to my shock that I detested some of the people I was living with. For years afterwards I wrestled with the feelings of hatred and loathing I had for these people. How could this be? I was, after all, a decent bloke and one of those nice Christians. We don't hate people; we love them, don't we? The Bible says I should. However, the reality of what I was genuinely like was starting to crash in on me. I was forced to admit I really did hate these people. I dreamed of returning there and sorting their community out! I wrestled with these feelings. I did my best to smother them. After all, having feelings like this was sinful.

This was the first time that my mask really began to slip. Up to then I had been a nice Christian. I had prayed, read the Bible and gone to church. I had done all the stuff you are supposed to do. OK, so the desire to do evangelism and the willingness to give to people without reward wasn't there, but I had tried, hadn't I? I was totally at a loss to know what God was up to. I had prayed about serving Him, and He led me to this community. But I hated it. The feelings made no sense. God didn't make sense. Neither was my faith making sense.

None of the straightforward rules I had learnt made sense any more. Where was God? Why wasn't He answering me? Why wasn't He making sense of this experience for me? Why wasn't He making it like it had been before I joined this community? Before, I had felt I could pray, and He would answer. But when I joined this community, after seeking his guidance, it felt like He had deserted me. I didn't feel close to Him any more. My prayers didn't get answered. I felt as if He had abandoned me. By this time it was the mid-nineties and I had spent several years knotted up, hating these people. My faith was on hold and nothing made sense. Things were bad, but then they started to get really bad.

Three things happened at the same time in 1995 which really started to pull me apart. First, I started a Social

Work Diploma course. The course required me to look at my values, and work out how I came by them. I found this very destabilizing, unnerving. Secondly, I started a course in church looking at the issue of bereavement. My father had died a few years before, and I thought it would be useful to work through some of the issues. This opened me up to deep feelings that I didn't realize I had, including those about my brother's death. Then thirdly, I found myself experiencing feelings of lust of such powerful intensity that I had no idea how to deal with them. All in all it wasn't a good time for this nice Christian bloke, who was beginning to come apart at the seams.

For a few years I tried to deal with what was happening to me. I had prayer from people in church and also went for counselling. There was some help. Then I had some more pictures that flashed through my mind. One was of someone in the basement of a house. He was all alone, his heart was broken, he was in the dark, crushed by despair and hopelessness. Another picture was of a wild beast in a cage, suspended in mid-air by elasticated ropes. Despite all his howling he couldn't shake the cage loose. As I considered this second picture I realized I didn't want him to get loose either!

Although they seem obvious to me now, at the time I found it difficult to link these images to myself. Despite all the praying, laying-on of hands and trying to believe particular Bible verses for strength, nothing made any difference. For a long time I had wanted to hear that all the pain in my life was the work of demonic forces, and that all I had to do was to have really spiritual people pray really spiritual prayers for me. It would then all be over. Despite such prayer, at the core of my being nothing was changing.

Eventually I heard about the community in Deal and

got myself along to a workshop in 2001. What drove me there was the issue of lust. I could neither deal with it nor control the reaction inside me. I went looking for a quick fix for the pain of lust, but nothing that they said at the workshop seemed likely to fix me quickly. I heard about facing up to the choices I had made, taking responsibility for my life, dealing with reality and facing one's pain. However, talking to the men in the workshop provided me with a belief that *something* was working in their lives. These seemed to me to be real blokes, men without pretence or falseness. They didn't seem to me to be nice in the way I normally saw men in the church. In fact, there was a distinct lack of niceness in them, and a growing unnerving realization that I would probably have to stop being nice, and instead start getting real with myself, if I was going to sort myself out.

Over the next few months and years, I did my best to work with the teaching from the workshops. I attended a few more and diligently did my homework. Homework is time out to listen to God, hearing what He wants to say to you. As I listened to the talks in the different workshops, I started to hear about the idea that we have an elaborate network of defences in place to stop us getting near the truth or its pain in our lives. Some of our defences are unknown to us. Some of them we don't see as defences, but just as the way we have always lived our lives. It took me quite some time to grasp this idea. Unfortunately for me, I had never really considered where my strategies for life, such as they were, came from.

But as I pressed on with my homework I did begin to find all sorts of strategies and ways of thinking in place, designed to stop me facing my pain and to stop me getting real. For instance, I realized that I had an arrogant but unconscious view that my take on life was actually quite insightful and accurate. Similarly, I had an unacknowledged view of my relationship with God as very insightful, with which He was quite impressed. I also believed I had a position in His sight above other more ordinary sinners. This level of unreality was a very effective way of warding off suggestions or information that did not conform to this standard. How could I hear that I was an ordinary sinner, or that my life-view was part of my problem, if I unconsciously believed otherwise? Only when I became aware of these views that I carried could I begin to acknowledge that not only were these views of mine wrong, they were embarrassing in their self-importance.

But none of these views were ever consciously verbalized in my mind, let alone acknowledged openly to others. I gradually learnt that I had many such unacknowledged attitudes and assumptions in my life. As I began to probe them, one of the first things I realized, when I stopped arguing with myself, was that I didn't want to change a thing. I had started to admit to having failings, but I had no motivation to change them. However, the physical pain I carried reminded me of the necessity to develop some motivation. I also became aware of how frightened I actually was about probing into my history and becoming aware of the pain I carried.

Slowly and gradually it dawned on me what my life strategy really was. As a child, I should have been racked with grief and shock at losing my beautiful little brother. So should everyone else in my family. But at that time there was little awareness in society of the need for adults to talk about grief and bereavement, let alone children. My father was unable to cope, so he effectively banned all of us from mentioning this loss. Unfortunately, sadness does not go away just because it is ignored, nor does time heal all our wounds, but we all tried to bury our sadness.

My solution, as a four-year-old, completely understand-able at the time, was to hide it away. And I had done this ever since.

It is strange that as I grew up I never reversed the decision I had made to repress and deny what had happened. But having made it, with pressure from those around me, I began to own the decision as my own. The decision grew into a determination to protect myself from ever experiencing any pain like this again. I couldn't possibly allow this much pain to hurt me again. I hid my pain and emotion in the basement of my spiritual house, but didn't realize it. I had caged my fury so that it would never escape, so that I wouldn't have to feel the molten lava of its rage.

If I was going to hide my emotion away, without realizing it, I would also need to deal with everything such emotion was linked with. So I removed myself from both my family and all other people. This initiative was designed to protect me from the pain involved in loving people and getting close to them.

All of this meant I was deciding never to allow myself to get close to another person and thereby experience such pain again. My decision took me away from others and meant that I began to live life in isolation. I would be safe on my own because I had no other choice. I had to protect myself. No one would be able to hurt me again, and the price I paid was that I would never love or be loved again. Like my father I still existed, but the human, warm part of me was banished. I became a dutiful child, eager to please. I could obey rules. I became the elder son in the Prodigal Son story. I worked, I studied, but I was removed from human contact.

One of the most difficult points in my journey has been the realization that I am responsible for my life. Not my father or mother. Not my priest or my vicar. My life is my responsibility. I am the one who can make and unmake my life decisions. So I found myself with all this information about what had happened and what I had done with it. As a child I had made a decision, a means of surviving a trauma, but I had never intended the consequences. I had cut myself off from all help, human and divine. I had lived a fearful, lonely life. And now, in my late forties, I was coming apart at the seams. I didn't realize it at first, but all the pain, rage and bitterness of my childhood experiences were still there. It took a long time to come to the realization that regardless of whether or not I could blame anyone else for the pain I suffered, I was now responsible for all the consequences. Now what was I going to do, to make or unmake all these decisions? The realization dawned that I do have the ability to choose; I have the power to act in my life. So I began to make new and different choices. After many fearful false starts I began to allow myself to feel the hidden pain. I cried and wept for the loss of my beautiful little brother. I grieved the loss of the fun and delight of having another brother in my life.

On one occasion I was with two men from the community in Deal in a makeshift troika, a group of three supporting each other. I was grappling with how unfair it all was. Why had none of my relatives thought I needed comforting? In the middle of all my tears one of the men asked who I was angry with. Eventually, out of the confusion of my pain the answer bubbled up: 'him'. My little brother. I was angry with my little brother. I had loved him with all my four-year-old heart, and he had deserted me. He had gone away and left me. Ten weeks old, yet I was angry with him! This was both a shock and a revelation to me, but I could not deny it. Here I was in my forties with the feelings of a four-year-old. How could this be? It didn't make sense. But it was true. I had buried those feelings, perhaps out of shame and embarrassment. But there it was. Feeling it and allowing it to surface out of me brought a deep sense of relief. I was beginning to get real, even though real didn't make rational sense to my university-trained mind. But it did make emotional sense. It was all there. I had just chosen to hide it.

As I let myself have these feelings that I had hidden for so many years, other things also began to happen. I began to sense that rather than tormenting me, God had been beside me all my childhood life. He had stayed with me in my grief, in the cold, damp house I had grown up in. I had hated Him and feared Him, but He had stayed with me and shared my grief. I had been unaware of this. 'I was senseless and ignorant; I was a brute beast before you.' In time I began to feel sad, thinking of Him, feeling such deep sorrow for so long. Rather than God having been remote and indifferent towards me, I had actually been the cause of sadness to Him. It is quite a shock to think that your life can cause Him pain, but mine clearly had.

You will have noticed that throughout my story I have been referring to Him as God. This is a very remote way of addressing Him. Gradually and slowly I have started to develop the courage and genuine belief that I can call Him Father. I am beginning to sense that what he feels for me is not duty, but a genuine affection and fondness. I am beginning to allow myself to let Him and others close. I am experiencing many more feelings about everything. Although this is not comfortable, I do know this is life, and I would rather have it than live the kind of life I had previously chosen for myself.

This has only been one part of my story. As I continue my journey, I am discovering there are many other issues that I need to address. But now it is a journey with my

Father, one we are taking together at a slow, gradual pace. I am learning to say to my Father with assurance, 'You hold me by my right hand. You guide me with Your counsel, and afterwards You will take me into glory.'

Some Comments

Martin and Liam were both shocked to discover the depth of the emotion they carried. This is typical of most men's journeys. We deny we are emotional and close ourselves down, but over the years the toxic pools of emotion build, eventually biting us back with physical illnesses, psycho-physiologically driven (that is, driven in part by the emotion in our body, but which we deny). All men are emotional, just as women are, but culturally as westerners we refuse to live this emotion. We see throughout the Old Testament that Hebrew man was emotional, but we deny it. What becomes clear to all men, as they begin to give the Lord and themselves permission to let the emotion surface, is that emotion is not an enemy they must suppress but a colourful ally on the path to healing. It's a huge asset.

The New Testament, likewise, supports the idea that emotion is an ally. For instance, most of the times when Jesus speaks of the Holy Spirit, He does so in emotional terms, e.g. the Comforter, the Counsellor. But the failure of much western Christianity is that people do not *feel* they know God. We must all learn to emotionally engage with God, not least because much spiritual gifting is first felt, not thought. Also, although loving is a thing we deliberately choose to do, in practice love, to be lived, must be emotionally alive. Emotion gives life to our lives.

One of the other big areas for both Martin and Liam was their need to admit the damage they had done to themselves in trying to cope with and control their pain. Martin used his learnt knowledge of the world of women to manipulate and control all those around him. Liam chose to bury his pain and isolate himself. As a result of these early choices, each became very different from the person they were created to be. But what became apparent to both of them was the need they had to admit this is what they had done. On our journey we all have to learn that although what has happened to us was bad, what we have done with it turns out to be far more damaging.

The issue of personal responsibility is a huge area for men, as it is for women. We know that someone is beginning their journey in earnest when they say something like, 'I am my problem, aren't I?' or 'I've really screwed up, haven't I?' By admitting we are the problem, we are also admitting that we have in our hands the capacity to do something about it, with the Lord's help. Personal positive change is God's *Rapha* gift to all of us. He wants to meet us in our pain, not just in our triumphalism.

What also becomes clear is that the Lord has for many years been one of the many spectators in our lives, looking on at the way we are hurting ourselves. As we begin our journey He will have much to say about what has happened, and what we have done, but He will say none of this until we have earned the right to this knowledge by our commitment to the journey. Also, He needs to see us reach a place where what He says will not be too shocking to us, or so off base that we say it's the Enemy talking! His perspective on our disorders is often outside the box.

One final comment. Men have been leaving the church in their tens of thousands in recent years. Here in the UK, the ratio of membership overall is now a clear two to one in favour of women. Church is becoming a women's club. The reason why many men back off is simple. Their Christianity no longer has any relevance to the life they are living throughout their week. Also, they can see few good reasons for being a Christian. Many men go to church just because their wives do. What we have found in CCD and *Rapha* is that men will follow Christ, and it will make sense, if they are able to see that He is for them and wants them to become the person He created them to be, not merely expecting them to remain the person they have become.

Notes

[1] Martin is describing several steps in a typical journey. People will often start by beginning to acknowledge the damage done to them by others, both the important and the apparently insignificant. But this leads them to explore how they have responded to that damage, the coping mechanisms they put in place, and the damage they did to themselves as a result.

[2] Though some may have a theological problem with this idea, it is common for people to sense and hear the Lord saying sorry for what may have happened to them. Many will also have a sense that the Lord was present in those difficult, traumatic moments. This can help them counter the common accusation of many concerning where God was when they were being raped, being abused or hurting, etc.

[3] A righteous brokenness is a place we all need to reach as men, where we are no longer arrogant or self-righteous, but sensitive to others' needs, mellow in personality and aware of our own humanness.

[4] It's interesting to ask whether this was an attack of the Enemy or whether the Lord allowed it as a way of speaking to Martin. But the question is irrelevant, as it was not the

incident that was the test, but how he responded to it. As a result, he was able to tell everyone that he could not be a builder or soldier any more, but only the new Martin in Christ.

5

Mental Illness

We have many people who are part of our community or who have attended our workshops who did not realize the extent of their need. People like Derry, Nicola, Liam, Martin – each would have considered themselves relatively healthy. For many of us, our Christianity is a way of proclaiming our well-being rather than a platform to tell the world how sick we really are from the disease called sin. We are even in danger of giving false testimony, feeling a need or pressure to defend God and be positive, rather than admitting how bad 'bad' really is. God has so much more to redeem in all of our lives, in this life, than most of us are willing to admit.

Since many people in the church think they are OK, we have found ourselves working with those who know they are not. Two of these groups are those with addictive or mental health disorders, in either their past or their present. These are the ones unable to maintain a 'healthy' life. Even before CCD, this had become a specialist side to our work, supporting those who either want to break one or more of the hundreds of addictive disorders or have experienced mental illness. In this we feel we are following Christ's command, to go to the sick and poor (Mk. 2:17, Lk. 11:5ff.

and 14:13, 21, etc.). (Poverty often accompanies mental illness.) Mental illness is not an unusual problem. In the UK, every year one in four adults will suffer some type of mental illness.[1]

Coming back from addictions or mental or emotional illness is a hard path to walk. But what we have learnt is that much of the time as those who are most damaged become healed, breaking the cycles of sickness in their lives, they turn out to be some of the most gifted people in the community. Another thing we have noted is that often those who are most sick are the most desperate to find healing. They recognize their need and are most willing to change. They will pay the great price. Many, we find, have given up ever believing they could be well.

Another reason I believe the Lord has led us in the way He has is that it is almost as though, in our early years, the Enemy is able to see our potential in Christ and seeks to damage us as much as he can, before we ever move into relationship with Christ. Much addictive disorder and mental illness is debilitating. It becomes a useful tool to permanently harm us. So in CCD and *Rapha* we have a disproportionately high number of people with such backgrounds, who with the Lord's help and mentor support are able to recover from their dark pasts. Let us look at two typical cases.

Breaking the Cycle
Roman von der Goltz

I'm 30 years old, from Munich in Germany. I'm married to Rachael. Although I moved to Deal four years ago in order to join the community, in many ways I feel as if I have only just joined. I used to be in social work but have now started my career as a management consultant. I'm really enjoying it. I love sport – every sport really.

They call it 'substance abuse' but it was not the substance I abused. It was myself, wasting my potential, not being there for a friend because I was stoned, killing myself slowly. Now I am starting again to hope and dream. I want to give myself life.

I was lying in my bed yesterday and saw a picture of myself running around in the kindergarten. I was always a kind of leader; I really enjoyed it, and I was totally happy in there. I was in touch with people and was there for them. People looked up to me, even at that young age.

The next thing I saw was me being very lonely. My parents divorced when I was 7 and from then on I can't remember much of my childhood. I felt responsible for the divorce. And that's when it started. I felt ashamed all the time about myself and what I'd done, in allowing the divorce to happen.

I remained with my mother. That was a very hard decision. They asked me who I wanted to go with, my father or mother. To make this decision when you are 7 is not the easiest thing in the world. I think perhaps I felt bad about my father, but I can't really remember. I think I just blocked it out.

From then on I just got more and more unhappy and distant. I definitely lost what I had had as a child. I used to be happy, always making contact with people, talking, just enjoying being with people, being with myself. I lost all of that. Now I am beginning to believe I can get it back. I am discovering ways to find the person I was meant to be.

Looking back, I can see I changed a lot during my time at school. We moved around a lot. I changed schools ten times. Every time I started making friendships, six months later we were moving again. So I thought, 'Hey, why bother doing something like that again?'

I remember my grandmother and my great-aunt. I imagine they'd lived together forever. They just stood with the Lord all their life, but they never preached at me. It was amazing to see how they could go through all the wartime, losing friends and family, and just be happy. In their home in Germany they talked about all their experiences, more and more despair and death. But they always saw the Lord guiding them. I see now how amazing it was, but then they were just nice people to be around, people who didn't feel ashamed. It was just good to be there – playing cards, having a meal, sitting in the garden. I can now see that they had a big influence on me.

When I was 13 or 14, I decided to go and live with my father. Immediately my mother got ill – it might have been a heart attack. I remember the ambulance coming, and my stepfather blaming it all on me, saying, 'It's your fault your mother's nearly died.'

So I went to my father, going to school near him. I found a new girlfriend, so it was OK for a year or two. But after that we broke up. I knew the area well, and had known many people there all my life, so it was easy for me to slip away, to go somewhere and not be home for two or three days, even though I was only 15. I found people doing drugs. It wasn't a problem, because my father was drunk a lot. He assumed I was with friends, if he thought at all. He didn't care if I came home at midnight, or four in the morning.

I don't know, maybe it was just the area we lived in, but everyone seemed to be taking drugs. In the beginning I didn't use it to harm myself, or to get away from stuff I couldn't handle. That came later. At first it was a way of making friends, like those I'd had when I was a child, before the divorce. Not entirely the same, but similar. When you were doing drugs you were usually with people, because where the drugs were the people were. You had a good time.

Most of them were using the drugs to shut down the feelings regarding their state: 'I'm not working,' 'I'm not good at school,' 'I have problems at home.' You're all on the same level. There's no shame if everyone's taking drugs – you're not ashamed that you do it. But increasingly these are the only people you are around, because when you meet friends not doing drugs you're ashamed of who you are becoming.

I always felt too tall. On the other hand I was always successful in sports, in soccer, in American football. I wanted to go to a college in America to play there, so I would be one of the first German people ever to go over to America and play football. That was my ambition. But then I injured my knee and ripped all my ligaments. After that I lost even my drive to do sports, and found myself more and more just hanging out with friends doing drugs. But I was never really a heavy drug user, just enough to blow away everything that I didn't want to remember. I never did hard drugs.

Just before I came to England for the first time I was admitted to a psychiatric hospital, but that wasn't the answer. Yes, I was depressed, but I didn't think I was mentally ill. I just didn't care any more. After I injured my knee I lost a great deal of weight. I stopped eating and my weight nearly halved. I didn't eat for weeks – just chocolate. I was living upstairs in a flat with two cats messing all over the place. I didn't care any more.

My friend came to see me on my birthday and said, 'Hey, you need help.' So he took me to the hospital, which was nice because they took care of me. Everything was done for me, while they tried to blame mental illness or something else. I enjoyed it in there, but I was never really mentally ill. I had voices in my head, but I knew where they came from. I just didn't care where I was any more. It didn't matter.

I was sedated half the time and everything was blamed on some physical or mental cause. I knew I wasn't mentally ill, but I was beginning to admit something was not right. They were not helpful in there, so I was happy to be out. Then I had a social worker with me, which didn't last long. They don't stop telling you how to manage your life – but it didn't work.

I came to England and began talking to Peter. 'He's just another stupid psychiatrist,' I thought. But it was different. It was the first time I decided to trust somebody, and it just opened up. I didn't have a choice really, because he told me straight what was going on with me. Peter understood what I was talking about, and because of that I couldn't run any more.

I originally came for a sort of holiday, a long weekend with my future father-in-law. He visited his old friend Peter, and suddenly I found myself in a workshop, from Friday to Sunday. Wow! And that was it, even with my broken English! Come Sunday, after the workshop, I broke down and then slept on the way from Deal to the airport, in the airport, on the aeroplane and on the truck back, finally crawling into my bed and sleeping through till the next morning!

My first choice was to stay in Germany and live there like everybody else, but that would be to repeat the history of my father, doing just what he had done. I decided I did not want to just repeat history any more. I wanted to live my own life, have a future. When I got back to Germany I sensed something was missing. I didn't know what, but I had left a piece of myself back in England, a part of me that people in Germany couldn't touch. So I had to go back, because now I felt worse than ever before![2] I couldn't even keep down the drugs; it was no longer possible. Something was missing, even though I was with all my friends and doing all the usual stuff – it was not the same any more. So I had to go back to Deal.

I was engaged to Rachael, now my wife. Rachael was everything to me. She was the one who basically kept me going. She had known me for seven years. We met when she was cheerleader for the football team and got to know each other, but she split up with me and went to America for a year, which was a really bad time for me. She came back, however, and now we're married. But so determined was I, I would have come to the UK even if she wouldn't come with me.

In England there was something else that had touched me for the first time, which nobody else could have understood. But it wasn't words. I had never experienced it before. It gave me just a second of peace, of hope that things could be different. I couldn't put it into words, but something was touching me. I became aware of this because my head was normally full of voices. I was always seeing things, sensing stuff. I sensed people's moods, and could manipulate them if I wanted to, just by seeing what was going on.

In Deal they taught me some of this was spiritual, and that was OK by me. In the past I'd thought, 'You're just an idiot.' But I could always feel there was more. And I didn't want to believe that's all there was, just carbons and proteins, that Rachael was nothing more than strings of nerves and tissue. I knew there was more. I'd seen it in other people, felt it in other people. But I was never really into Jesus, God or anything like that. I had gone to church a little in Germany, but they were not touching what people were touching when I came to Christ Church. In the past I'd felt so different, never really blending in with anyone. But I came here and everybody was into it, everybody was touching this spiritual, God place. I no longer had to be different; I didn't have to hide.

We were arranging our wedding in Germany, and I returned to Deal for much of that time. I stayed with a couple in Deal for a week, which stretched to two weeks, then three, at which point my boss sent me a fax saying, 'You're fired'. Then it was four and five weeks. I almost stayed to the start of my wedding. I finally returned to Germany and a week later we married, but a week after that we moved to England. It was only then that it became clear to me what a massive change it would be to live here in England. I panicked and began doing stupid things, like leaving Rachael.

I remember imagining just jumping in my car and going back to Germany for a weekend or so, going over to Holland and smoking pot there, and then realizing why I had moved over here. It took quite a while before I started settling in. I left Rachael much of the time, going off to Germany and coming back.

I began to build relationships, just a few. I don't know what it was, but here in the UK I had to start making decisions. In Germany I didn't care, and I still didn't care here really, but I started making some decisions. I started meeting with other men. It becomes much harder to live your old life when everybody knows what you're doing, and people begin telling you all the potential and gifting you have. Then you realize you can't have both your old life and your future – that's not possible. But it took me three-and-a-half years living here in Deal to realize this.

I fought every inch of the way, but I began to notice that every time I dealt with an issue in my life I stopped using drugs for a time. Then they would come back again. I was deciding what was good, so I had to make new decisions about where to go from here. Do I really want it? And always, just as I was making the decision, knowing this was the best thing for me to do, I would start doing drugs again.

So I continued using drugs while telling people, 'I don't want to go there, I will never go there.' I didn't want to do homework because I knew I would have to deal with the drugs. I would have to face the decision to give myself life: 'Yes, I want to work. I really want to have a working life.' So I began to earn money, to support Rachael. When I took to the drugs I didn't want to support Rachael or myself. But why wouldn't I want to do that? As I did the journey, too many issues surfaced, so I began using drugs again.

I always knew, however, that it was never really about drugs. Drugs were just a symptom of the decision to give myself life or not to care. If I made the decision to give myself life, drugs were not an issue. I never had any withdrawal symptoms or anything like it. Whether or not I did drugs was dependent on the decisions I made. If you make the decision to give yourself life, a lot of responsibility comes with it. But if you say no and take drugs, it's a nice excuse: 'I'm stoned and I don't want to meet people, don't want to face it. If it gets any worse, hey, I just smoke more weed.'

It was good in Germany because nobody really cared. But here in the community you can't live like that, you can't isolate yourself like that. There are people, all the time, drawing out who you really are, who you can be. It now hurts much more than before when I take drugs. It just hurts, because I can see what I am destroying when I do it. The difference now is that I have a choice. When I was in Germany I didn't really have a choice. In Germany my choice was, 'Be in pain or take drugs.' But now it's, 'Do I want to repeat history, or do I want to have a future?'

Before, I couldn't handle the decisions, reaching out for the opportunities: the risk that I could fail or succeed, or just lose it. So for me the easy option was to say, 'Oh, I can't do it anyway, so leave it,' and take more drugs.

Using drugs was just a way to harm myself, to put myself down. With every opportunity I wasted, I wanted to hurt myself more, so the best way was taking drugs, killing myself slowly. But I have to say it's much more painful here because you know that what was happening wasn't fake, you know it's working if you want it to. And if you want it, everything is there for you. For example, I started dreaming again. I never dreamt before, when I was in Germany, except about all the things that could go wrong. It had taken me years to see how I was abusing myself, but now I was seeing it in two or three weeks. That's the difference now. But it was still the same cycle. You have to make a decision: I can take this opportunity and give myself life, or I can avoid it and go back into abusing myself with drugs. Every time a decision came, I pushed it away. Another lost opportunity.

Now I am starting to learn to break this cycle. If I have a decision to make, but instead abuse myself, I now watch myself doing it and begin saying sorry straight away. So it now only takes a week or two before I again reach the point of saying, 'Yes, that's it. OK, I'm going for it. This is my decision.' I still have to fight it. If something comes up, the most convenient thing is still to get something to smoke, or close myself down, or isolate myself.

When I'm back in Germany my decisions are so much harder, because there is nobody standing with me. They don't understand the decisions I've made, and why. The choices that I make here, yes, they're still hard to keep to, but because other people are moving on as well, doing the same thing, doing the journey, it's much easier, if you go wrong, to go to somebody and get affirmation. Yes, you made a mistake, but the world's not going under. So try it again.

The most difficult thing for me is still to say sorry to myself. I still have to practise it time and again. Just to forgive myself, to say to myself that I'm worth a new beginning when I've made a mistake, that it's OK to make mistakes but you have to say sorry to yourself. And I think that's one of the main reasons why I took drugs. I was never able to say sorry to myself. 'It's always my fault' and 'It will not happen for me' was all I knew. When I say sorry to myself, it just goes: I don't have to take drugs, or put myself down. When I say sorry, I give myself permission to make a new beginning.

These days I am able to say, 'Well done, Roman!' And it's a very nice feeling when you can look in the mirror and say, 'Thank you, Roman. Well done!' There's just so much peace and happiness inside. The hope that you're no longer cursed to repeat history, and that there is a future if you want it. But the 'take it or leave it' decision is still mine.

Living with Depression
Fiona Burman

I'm 34, am married to Ray (we got married last year) and have a teenage son. I was born in north Scotland and lived there until five years ago, when I moved to Deal. I have just graduated from university with a degree in Social Policy and will start an MA in Journalism next year.

I come from a large family, as did my parents. Mum was one of six and Dad was one of five. I was also one of five, with four younger brothers. When I was very young we moved down south for a few years before heading back up to Scotland in the late 1970s. From this time on we lived on a farm that belonged to my mother's family, and that is where I grew up. My Dad worked hard to support us all, while Mum was kept busy with a young family to look after. Dad worked for the local landowners (my grandparents) and the family estate was where my parents had first met. Their backgrounds were in such stark contrast to one another. Dad was working-class and Mum came from a landed family. I have always felt more at ease in the company of my father's family, and always felt I wasn't quite good enough for my mother's side.

My parents and some members of my wider family were Christians. But when I looked at most Christians there seemed a contradiction between what they preached and what they practised. From my perspective, it became a powerful tool whereby they could use everything in the name of God to punish and control me. For example, I came home late one night, and as a result I was made to go to church. It felt as if church was the punishment for bad behaviour. The meetings I was dragged to seemed very false through my childish eyes, and I grew to hate my parents and God for what I felt. Surrounded by so much religiosity among my family, I became consumed by guilt and shame for everything I did. I lived in a constant state of fear, believing that the world was about to end and I would go straight to hell. My perception of God was not as a loving father, but as a spoilsport ready to punish you if you so much as thought a wrong thought. That ended Christianity for me!

While we did have some happy times together as a family, from my perspective at least these times seemed rare and fleeting. Life in a male-dominated environment (I had four brothers) was loud and noisy more often than not. Home was a place where emotions ran riot. It felt as if everything was on the surface, with lots of mocking, anger, arguments and tears, but I remember little love and understanding. Attempts at affection were usually clumsy and awkward, making everyone feel uncomfortable, so it was easier to do it quickly, make a joke out of it or not bother at all. I have few recollections of seeing my parents hug or kiss each other, and even when they did show affection towards each other, I'd feel as uncomfortable as they did; it was as though they were doing something abnormal. When my parents divorced, in the early 1990s, it affected us all deeply, but in very different ways. When you are young you imagine that your parents will 'live together happily ever after', but adulthood brings a reality that puts a full stop to unrealistic childhood hopes and dreams.

I am not aware of ever feeling depressed as a child;

lonely, yes, but not depressed. The first time that I was aware of feeling depressed was in my early twenties. At the age of 18 I became pregnant. This came as a huge shock to me, as I hadn't planned on having children, and certainly not at this point in my life. However, I decided that I would have my baby and accepted that single parenthood was now par for the course.

My life became mapped out for me there and then, so I moved into my own place and made a home for the two of us. Although I loved my son dearly, it was tough being a single parent. Living on the breadline and feeling very lonely triggered off the first of many bouts of depression. It was during this period in the early 1990s that I plucked up the courage to tell my GP how I felt. I was prescribed anti-depressants. This was to be the first of many visits.

From this period onwards, until the time I contacted Christ Church Deal, my life felt like a disastrous series of events, with each episode pushing the depression deeper and making me even more sick. I didn't realize this at the time, and convinced myself that I was a survivor, that I could take on all that life threw at me. I had such a defiant attitude, and was fiercely independent. What was the point of relying on others?

People always let you down, anyway. Or at least this is the conclusion I arrived at during this stage of my life.

In order to survive, I became increasingly hardened to all the pain, even though I was in turmoil on the inside. I was growing very angry and bitter, and my violent outbursts usually got the better of me as I became aggressive at the smallest thing. I was a time bomb waiting to explode. I could not understand why I carried such a rage, but the pain inside was so raw that it was a battle to keep it suppressed.

In my many attempts at controlling how I felt, I became obsessed with keeping my home clean. Dirt and mess made me deeply anxious, though I had been this way for as long as I can remember. Once my home was spotless, I felt good about myself for a short while.

Eventually, my life revolved around keeping everything immaculate and in order. This part of my life I could control. However, having a young child running around meant I was constantly cleaning and tidying, getting very anxious when friends came over, in case they messed up my 'perfect' home. Towards the end, I didn't get many visitors. People could not relax in such a state of perfection, and I didn't want to see anyone anyway. However, I hated being so driven. How on earth could I stop? I tried at a conscious level to relax more, cutting down on the amount of cleaning I did. But this didn't work, because I panicked if anyone tried to stop me fulfilling my obsessive rituals.

In stark contrast to my independent streak was the desperate need to have a boyfriend. I felt as though I couldn't be a whole person unless I was in a relationship. Even if the relationship was a disaster, it was preferable to loneliness. I had no shortage of men; the trouble I had was keeping them. In my longest relationship we were together for four years. During this time I was involved in drugs. At last, I found something to control my erratic feelings. Drugs made me feel confident, giving me a sense of belonging. They also helped me relax in the company of others, something I really struggled with. I felt so rotten most of the time that getting high helped me feel better, albeit temporarily. The police searched our home for drugs on more than one occasion but instead of that being a warning, it merely encouraged us to find better places to hide our stash.

However, this became a very abusive relationship, ending tragically. One of the most painful experiences was when I saw my boyfriend having a sexual relationship with someone in my family. This was the ultimate betrayal. The abusiveness of this devastated me. I increased my intake of anti-depressants and mixed them with alcohol to help cope with the trauma it triggered inside me. We split up, but several months later we got back together. I was so desperate for acceptance that I tolerated being treated like trash.

Then came the final straw. I felt that he was seeing someone else again. As it happened, my feelings were confirmed. This someone else turned out to be the girlfriend of another member of my family. The two of them ran away together, leaving a trail of devastation, which resulted in the suicide of one of the few men in my family that I really trusted. My pain was unbearable. This was the beginning of the end for me.

My medication increased again, and I tried to cope with the pain I felt by keeping busy at home and at work, but inside I was dying. I moved house again, and this time I began getting pain in my arms. I put it down to stress, and was given even more medication. I was also finding it hard to sleep at night, so I began taking sleeping pills. My appetite went, and I lost a lot of weight. I didn't realize I was having a nervous breakdown. I thought that once I had settled in my new home, I would pick up again. Instead I became worse.

My friends and family couldn't handle it, telling me to pull myself together. I couldn't. I stopped washing myself, my home became a tip, my hair began to fall out, and my periods stopped. All I could do was stare out of my prison at the life that went on around me, wanting so desperately to be a part of it, but unable to be. I had completely shut down. A psychiatric nurse came round most days and tried to get me to eat and get dressed, but I had no desire to do so. My poor son didn't understand what was wrong. I told him I was ill, but would get better soon. He asked me every day if I was getting better. I wasn't, but I couldn't say that to him.

That was me when I first arrived at Christ Church Deal. I got in touch with them after a phone call from a relation who suggested it was worth a try. I came down to Deal twice, the first time to find out what help they could give me. Initially, I thought it wasn't for me, as I believed that if I got my flat back, I'd start feeling better. When I realized this made no difference, I came back down again. My son cried and screamed at me not to go without him, but I had to. We were reunited three weeks later when he arrived. All I wanted was to get well, to come out of the hell I was in. When I look back, getting to Deal was a miracle.

I had spent all of my twenties on medication, seeing counsellors or psychiatric nurses, but they had no answers to my questions. However, after spending time in counselling sessions at Christ Church, I started to discover the reasons for the mess I was in. It was explained to me that my medication controlled the emotional symptoms of deeper roots, and that I needed to engage the root of the pain I carried, so that I could become free of it. Initially, this completely baffled me, particularly when it was explained to me that toxic emotional pain had become embedded at the core of my being, and was now dictating both the way I lived and also my future. To put it simply, I had to get real about how I felt and get in touch with my feelings at an emotional level. I was taught in sessions how to let go of the years of pain and abuse that I had locked away inside myself. Finally, I was beginning to get some answers.

One of the areas I had to look at was the intense anger I felt towards my mother. This was a significant part of my depression and was causing me such bitterness. It is not socially acceptable or Christian to feel this way, but the truth was that this was eating away at me like a cancer. Although we never had a good relationship, I still felt guilty for feeling this way about her. However, once I started to be honest with myself, it became much easier.

From my perspective it seemed that my mother hadn't wanted me. Because of this, I spent many years feeling that I was a big mistake. I lived in fear of upsetting her and I felt angry that the relationship I so desperately wanted seemed impossible. It wasn't fair. It was as though there was an impenetrable barrier between us. This was heightened by my fear of saying the wrong thing. Any feelings or emotional connection that did manage to filter through felt tainted by hate, anger, mocking and rejection.

In my head I believed I had forgiven her for how I felt she had treated me, but who was I trying to kid? The pain I felt inside was as raw as the day it had been deposited in me. It took very little prodding, and each time it was all churned up I vowed I would never forgive her. It seemed as though I was somehow trivializing how I felt if I let go of the revenge.[3] Forgiving her was condoning it. However, I learnt that by holding on to it I kept the pain in place, so it became a continuous cycle, with the vengefulness being fed by the pain. I had to decide that I would give the revenge to God, as He could execute the right to revenge, not me. Also, I learnt that forgiveness would release me and that this would then become my protection. In order to do this I declared every day for a week that I wanted to let go of the revenge I carried, and give my pain to the Lord.

A week later it went. I had carried this all my life and now it was gone! I could hardly believe it had worked. When I awoke the next day, I felt so light. I went into the town and kept checking my bag was still on my shoulder, as I thought it might float away. It felt as if I had been carrying a heavy old rucksack on my back for many years, but now I had left it somewhere because I didn't need it any more. My expectations of my mother could no longer hurt me, because I had separated myself emotionally and spiritually from her and let her go. This meant that I could be the real me without all the demands and expectations previously required.

I had no realization of the true extent of the revenge I carried. It had become like a poison, draining the very life from me. No wonder I had always felt so tired and heavy. I wanted to kill my ex and the girlfriend he still had for the part they had played in the suicide of a close family member. Every time I even saw a car like the one they had I would begin trembling and feeling sick. But once I had declared I also wanted to let go of this revenge, the Lord took the pain in the same way. What I was experiencing was not a temporary fix. For instance, when I think about the suicide and the surrounding events, they remain fresh in my memory, but the toxicity of the pain has gone.

Another cause of my depression was the intense anger and hatred I carried towards myself. This was an all-consuming self-hatred, which attracted destructive relationships to me like a magnet. I was unconsciously inviting people to abuse me, because I thought so little of myself. I don't know if those who knew me could sense this, but I had become an expert at being someone I wasn't, because being someone else was easier and less painful. In my mind, if I was the real me, nobody would like me, and I would suffer more rejection. All I ever wanted was to be accepted and liked. I tried so hard to make people like me, to the point of completely binning myself and wearing other people's personas.

It took very little to trigger my self-hate, because I have always held such a low opinion of myself. So much so that if I lost my temper with my son, I would call myself horrible names and hit myself. I felt I had to punish myself for being such a cow.

Several months after moving to Deal I decided to get baptized. Not long after this occasion, someone laughed at me. No big deal, but because I had carried a great fear of being mocked for as long as I can remember, this small incident spiralled me into intense anger towards myself for being so stupid and useless. When I got home I drank myself into a stupor to drown the pain. This only further fuelled my rage. So I grabbed a pair of scissors, ran into the bathroom and started hacking my hair off until there was no more to cut. When I looked down, my hair was lying in chunks all over the floor. I looked into the mirror, screaming at myself, 'I hate you. You should never have been born.'

The declaration I had made by getting baptized threw up a massive conflict within me. It felt as though all hell had been let loose within me, as I either banged my head continuously against the wall or punched and slapped myself around the head. With such a history I had to make the decision that I would stand with Christ, and not with all the blackness that I had become. It became a daily battle, choosing to say sorry to myself for what I had done to myself, accepting that the Lord had forgiven me. That bit was easy. The difficult part was that I had to learn to forgive myself. I felt this was impossible. How on earth could I forgive myself? After all, I deserved it. I was a big mistake, so my life was a mess.

It was so hard to separate the real me from the false selves I had created in order to cover up the deep pain inside.[4] What helped was being with people who believed in the real me. These people showed me such love, and gave me such tremendous support during those dark times, that I don't think the change would have been possible without them. They could see my potential, even though I couldn't.

By saying sorry to myself and letting it go, I've found the drive to hurt myself has completely gone. I now realize I like myself, which is a miracle. This has been made even easier by my choosing to take responsibility for my life and making peace with all the other positive decisions I had made. While I have undoubtedly made lots of mistakes, they no longer haunt me.

Betrayal was a major contributor towards my depression. It was the story of my life. People always deserted me, and I couldn't understand why it kept happening. Was there something wrong with me? Just about everyone I had a relationship with betrayed me. It was a pattern that repeated itself throughout my life. Constant rejection doesn't do much for self-worth, so I started sleeping around in the hope that I would find someone to make me feel better about myself. However, this merely exacerbated how I already felt.

A few months after moving to Deal, I met someone else. It was a very intense relationship, and it didn't take long for this to deteriorate either. My worst fear was that he would find someone else, then leave me. He did. I was devastated and the pain was so unbearable that I thought I would never get over it. I even considered returning to the north of Scotland, so that I wouldn't have to see them together. When I heard they were getting married, it tore me apart. I don't think I had ever cried so much in my life. What was in me that invited all this betrayal? I was on my knees crying out to the Lord to help me, to show me why this kept happening, as I couldn't take any more.

I was shocked and sickened by what came next. The words 'sexual abuse' came into my mind and almost instantly I started to feel my body turn cold as I began to shake and tremble. I felt this was the Lord giving me an answer. Even though I had no memory or cognitive knowledge of this, my feelings were telling me a different story.[5] Whether a physical act had taken place or not was irrelevant. What mattered was that at an emotional level it felt as if it had happened and I had to acknowledge these feelings as an emotional reality in order to let them go. The more I thought about it, the more I realized that the shame I felt about my body, my obsession with cleanliness and my disgust at men could all have stemmed from this root. On this basis it was little surprise that my relationships with men never lasted. Simply because of the hatred I felt towards them, because of what I felt had been done to me.

As a consequence of this, I was unconsciously inviting more abuse by picking men who would do me the most damage. This in turn justified my hatred of them. I had to let go of all the hate I carried towards the men who had treated me with such contempt. More importantly, I had to say sorry to myself for the contemptuous way I had treated myself.

When I looked at the carnage of my life I realized that the biggest betrayal was what I had done to myself. My sin against myself.

Since I started this journey God has redeemed so much of what had been stolen. While it has been a long and difficult journey of self-discovery, I finally have some answers as to why I spent years on medication hoping that one day 'they' might discover a panacea to my personal hell. A large part of my depression and inevitable breakdown was due to the fact that I'd repressed so much. Instead of letting it out, I'd internalized it, blaming myself.

Looking back, I feel I have come a long way from the walking zombie who arrived in Deal at the beginning of 1999. That person is now a stranger, but now and again I catch a glimpse of her and I cry. Not tears of sadness, but tears of eternal thankfulness. Moving here saved my life and also gave my son a life. Since being here, I've got married, my education has been redeemed and for the first time I feel I have a future. My life is only beginning. It is a place where I was introduced to a real God, not one who is going to punish me, but instead a God who loves me and will never leave me. He has made me well and given me back more than I would ever have dreamt possible.

I wanted to share my story with you, as you read this book, for you to know that help is available. You do not have to stay imprisoned by the chains of your past. You can be free, in the true sense of the word. Free to be the person God created you to be.

Some Comments

Both Roman and Fiona had episodes of serious mental illness that were the direct result of the accumulation of years of emotional damage. We have found the most helpful approach in these situations is to begin dismantling the damage one step or layer at a time. Everyone's damage is unique. There are no formulas. So each individual needs the gentle hand and voice of God leading them step by step out of their sicknesses into wholeness. It is relationships that make most of us sick, so it needs to be relationships that help make us whole.

We do not specialize in mental illness or learning disorders caused by organic physical damage in the body. But even in situations like these we have been able to see significant improvement, if the person wants to positively change. The key with most such people is not the extent of the damage but the person's ability to comprehend change, a willingness to take responsibility, and the desire to change lifestyles and embrace patterns that welcome wholeness.

This choice is well illustrated in Roman's battle to make and adhere to the choice to change, instead of continuing to go for the easier option of his more familiar sicknesses and isolation. On this journey most people are shocked to discover how much they are actually in love with their sicknesses, seeing them as a 'friend' rather than as an enemy dismantling their lives.

Fiona describes the depth of her anger and revenge. Many people come to our workshops telling us they have forgiven the people who have abused them. We do not question this often very sincere belief. But instead we ask them if they have yet laid down their right of revenge, buried deep under the well-meaning idea of forgiveness. In laying down the revenge they are responding to the Lord, who asks them to give to Him their own righteous right to take revenge on the person at some time in the future, even if this were still possible. Only by such an act of trust in God, giving Him their right to revenge, will they be able to let the matter finally rest and get on with their lives.

The role of the community is particularly important for those whose healthy routines of caring for themselves have broken down. We all need the support of one another, but much wholeness on this journey is caught, not taught. Being around and meekly learning from people who are further down the road is essential if we are to be whole ourselves. So the more sick you are, the more you will need the support of those you can trust to lead you out of the maze of illness. In the following chapter we see how this works when we are confronting addiction disorders.

Notes

1. This horrific statistic comes from research undertaken by MIND.
2. When God first begins to speak to us about the damage in our life, it's not unusual for it to get worse rather than better. It is one of the side effects of beginning to look at ourselves from God's perspective and unpacking all that is hidden, rather than continuing to pretend. For many, it has to get worse before it gets better.
3. Many people seek to forgive but forget to lay down revenge. We have found in our work that a desire for revenge is a powerful emotion. Many people who have been deeply hurt discover this drive almost feels like a need – they need to avenge themselves, or someone they love, by taking revenge. It's an emotion we often do not realise we carry, but it can steal our capacity to forgive. When we let go of this emotional drive there are often very significant benefits.
4. The phrase 'false selves' is used in our work to describe the person we have sought to become, often in order to please others and put on happy positive masks for others. We are not suggesting all of our life is like this, but most of us will find that we need to discover these false selves if we are willing to know the truth.
5. It is more common than we are often prepared to admit that we bury trauma from our pasts deep inside us and 'forget'. But on our journey the Lord brings the feelings to the surface when we are ready to deal with them. Fiona was in danger of believing what she wanted to think, rather than following her feelings. Susan explores this issue further in her book, *Letting God Heal*, Authentic Media, 2004.

6

Addictions

Roman and Fiona both had diagnosed mental illnesses. But there are many of us whose lives betray serious damage without it ever reaching a diagnosed condition. *Rapha* and CCD are a journey suitable for anyone, from the very sick to those who simply feel the need for a tune-up. It is not just about getting healed but about getting whole by hearing God's voice and meeting Jesus. Many of us think addictions are signs of deep sickness. Sometimes they are, but most of us have addictions, whether we are willing to own them or not. For instance, television, caffeine, chocolate, our weight, our looks, even our relationship with God can be addictive/ compulsive. Susan Williams, for example, used churchgoing and the busyness of leadership as a way of hiding from her pain and trying to find acceptance.

The following three stories are about redemption from three difficult but different types of addiction. Steve's was an alcohol addiction, James and Christa had a serious addiction to spending, and Yvonne's was an addiction to self-hate. You will see they all have completely different backgrounds, but their histories created a need for each of them, which created the damage in their lives. In our community, our experience is that God expects to meet our unmet needs Himself, whatever they are. But for us to let Him do that, we first need the courage to find and own those needs deeply buried in each one of us. Only as we acknowledge such needs can Christ meet us in that place.

Dealing with My Addiction
Steve Mitchell

> *I'm 45 years old – you've met my wife Rebecca. I was born in Deal, although I was out of the country travelling for the first four years of my life because my father was in the Marines. When he died, we lived in Scotland before coming back to Deal when I was 15. At the moment I work in the transport industry. I've just completed a Diploma in Management.*

You go to work, you earn the money, you get drunk, you abuse everybody, you wake up with a hangover, you feel down, so far down you're suicidal. You have a drink, you feel better, you feel great. You then feel depressed. Round and round. I'd reached the depths, in the gutter I suppose, and I couldn't see a way out. I started to think, 'Well, there has to be something else. Why are we all here? What's this perpetual babies and growing up and having a look at the world? There's got to be something else, there's got to be.' That's when I started going to Peter.

At that time I was in a relationship with Rebecca, who is now my wife, which was nearly torn apart, and because I felt that this was the woman for me, that we were meant to be, I was going to fight for her. Part of me started the journey because I wanted Rebecca. And it was through her that I met Peter.

We were going through a bad time. I had huge credit card debts, I was gambling and drinking, and had a bad reputation at the golf club and other places as a bit of a lush, and it was all going wrong. But one of the things that I'd cottoned on to was this man's name – Peter. And it was Peter this, Peter that. So I was saying, 'Who is this Peter? Is this one of those sects? Are you being brainwashed?' No, no, no, and then I'd hear Peter again. So I said, 'I must meet this bloke.' And my intention was to tear him apart, or at least threaten him in no uncertain terms: If he tries to indoctrinate or change Rebecca, I'll be in there and I'll have him. I booked a time, and when I arrived I was welcomed into the front room. As I stood there waiting I had in my mind one of those American evangelists, 'Praised be the Lord' and all that, and I thought, 'Well, you can try that on me . . .' and in walked this short, greying, corpulent man (his words, not mine). This is Peter?

And I found a peace there, because I was very tired; my whole life was draining away. Even on that first time there I cried. I just felt something, something amazing – I felt I didn't have to pretend. It was as if somebody had taken a big coat off me and said, 'You can just relax, just let it all out.'

Here was this man who believed in God but actually, more importantly, believed in me. So I don't have to believe in God? Do I have to go to church? Not if you don't want to. How much is it going to cost me? Nothing. Here was a man and, as I found out, a community of people who would help me, do anything I wanted and not want anything back. But one thing made me angry at the time: 'I'm not here to save your relationships.' Then why are you here? Then the principle: 'We will help you to deal with your issues individually so that you become the person you should be, that you were meant to be, without all the baggage.' It took a while, but slowly I began to see what he meant.

From the earliest time my memories were of my mother drinking. Not every day, but all my memories are of the drink, the shouting, the abuse, waking me up, and as I got older I realized the extent of it. I was constantly phoned up by publicans or taxi firms on Friday and Saturday nights and I always had to go and pick her up off the bar, or out of the chair, and try to drag her into a taxi or carry her home. Some of the worst times were when men had followed her back and then I'd end up having a fight outside to stop them getting into the house.

I think my first memory is of following her from our house (she was drunk). She was trying to find my father and he'd gone down to play golf with his friends. I remember thinking she might get hurt, so I followed her. I thought it was miles, but it probably wasn't. I remember hiding in the woods and I saw her. She found him and she gave him a mouthful. I can't remember if she hit him, I don't think she did, but it was in front of all his friends and he had to drive her back. I was 8 or 9, and I hated her for doing that to my father.

I was 11 when my father was killed in a car crash by a drunk driver. My mother was thrown through the back window and got her leg crushed, which left her in hospital for about three months. It was like starting a new relationship with her, but she probably drank more after that and I suppose I can see why.

Peter said at one point that I was trying to revenge my mother: telling myself I could do the drink better than her. And I did: the life and soul of the party. You drink, you have a hangover: fine, no problem at all. I just went out, and that was fun. My first marriage happened because I was drunk one night. That's when I proposed. After a night out I was constantly having to phone up the next day to ask people what I'd done, to find out who I'd abused.

One of the biggest things I found was that I was a very demonstrative person. I'm very tactile, I like cuddles; I like to be loved. I suppose. I'm always known as a generous person, and I think part of that was trying to buy people's affection. My mother wasn't very affectionate, and if I didn't get the affection I would badger for it, I craved it. I suppose one of the worst times was when it wasn't going well with my first wife and I took an overdose. Obviously I failed in that one as well, because I woke up at 2 o'clock in the morning.

Then I got together with Rebecca and we would party; drink became a major issue in our lives. That's no way to have a relationship. We abused ourselves and each other with the alcohol and the party lifestyle. But then the children became affected. They started to see the drunkenness and the way we abused each other. Even though I had started the journey by then, and I was making progress, I hadn't really realized how big an issue alcohol was.

Last year I was best man at a friend's wedding and I was also the organizer of his stag night. I organized the meal and drinks, and more drinks. I was on quadruple drinks – two cream liqueurs and two whiskies in the same glass. I then apparently started crying through the evening. By the time I got home I was terribly gone. Some of the men came back with me. Rebecca was asleep and the children were in the house. There was an argument out the back and I hit one of the congregation from Christ Church. Then I went upstairs to Rebecca, stopped her getting out of the bedroom and verbally abused her for an hour and a half.

Earlier that day I'd had issues I was dealing with, and one of my friends said, 'Look, let's walk and talk about it: you need to get it out.' I said, 'No, I'll put it to rest tonight.' But the alcohol opened it all up. It just opened like Pandora's Box, or a can of worms, or whatever you want to call it, and everything came out. It started in the street, the emotion coming out. (I don't remember much of it; everyone else put the story together afterwards.) And then I remember waking up in the morning in another bedroom. I'd smashed stuff out the back, and when I woke up there was somebody asleep downstairs and somebody else asleep on the bathroom floor. So I'd not only abused our home, I'd brought other people back to abuse it. I'd scared the children, I'd physically abused one of the congregation and I'd terrorized Rebecca.

I phoned Peter that morning and he booked me in for a session straightaway. Peter already knew the full story and filled the gaps in my memory. Susan then came in and told me the awful things that I had said to Rebecca. It was quite unbelievable. It just felt as though my whole world was falling apart. All I could think of was that this was life or death. I said, 'I don't know where Rebecca is,' and Susan said, 'You don't realize that today she's actually doing her final presentation for her degree, which means today decides whether she'll get her degree or not?' I'd put her through all that abuse the night before, and she was doing a presentation in a local school, which was being filmed and graded.

She now has a new job; she did get her degree. But that round of events basically finished me off. Life or death, that's all I could see. If I didn't give up alcohol and deal with the issues, then that was it. I made the decision. I had to get up in front of the church. No, that's not how it was. I didn't have to: no one made me. But I wanted to, I had to, I had to open it up and let it all out, share it and apologize. And when I did it, I made sure the children were there as well, which was really hard.

I'd made the decision. It was time to go on a journey of really doing my homework, going back into my history and letting it all go, to the point where I could actually say sorry to my mother as I placed her on the empty chair. I was now facing the emotional and spiritual aspects of my addiction. I had a past which helped explain why I had become who I was.

I started to let go of my revenge. That's what I wanted: to hurt my mother. I hated her. And through the process I found all these feelings, the abuse that I'd had, all the stuff I'd done just to survive as an only child living with a mother who had drink problems. But then I had to realize that she didn't have the knowledge or the help that I've got. She went through part of the war, but what help did she have? She didn't have a Peter or Susan to say, 'We're here to help.' I know there was help, but not to the extent that we have now, and certainly not a therapeutic community like Christ Church.

So as well as finding all the anger and pain I carried, I had to start feeling sorry for my mother. That was a big turnaround for me. It meant getting rid of the vengefulness and the hatred, the wanting to hurt her, and actually stepping back and saying, 'Hey, what happened to her when she was young during the war and all the rest of it? That was really bad.' It was a love/hate conflict with her. I knew I had to say sorry to her.

One of the things we're taught to do as part of homework is, in your imagination, to place the person who has hurt you or done you harm in an empty chair and just tell them how you feel. Recently I had a headache for about nine-and-a-half weeks. I went to the doctor, I had blood tests, I thought I had a brain tumour (because I don't get many headaches). I went through every scenario, thinking of everything, taking different pills I don't like taking, to try to get rid of it, and it wouldn't go. In the end I thought, 'Well, homework? All right. In the chair. Let's try.'

I put my mother in the chair, and I let go of so much

emotion it hurt; it hurt spiritually and physically. In the end Mark, who was mentoring me, said, 'How does your head feel now?' 'Worse,' was my reply. I thought no more of it until about two days later, at work, when I realized the headache had gone. It had gone. I kept thinking, 'Why didn't I do that homework before?' I know it works, but then the doubts kick in. Is God real? Does homework really work? Although I know God's real, you have to believe it, you have to believe that God's there. I was kicking myself and smiling and thinking, 'Why didn't I just do the homework?'

Amazingly, I also found it easy not to drink. But one of the most astonishing things was that when I got up in church and said sorry, Rebecca just said, 'Thank you.'[1] And that's when our relationship really started, that day when I gave up. I did say that I wasn't going to drink ever again, but Peter suggested that was quite a big statement to make: 'There's nothing wrong with alcohol, like all things, in moderation.'

I had my first drink after that on our wedding night, back in our hotel. Everyone applauded as we went in and the barman offered us champagne. Rebecca said, 'Oh, that'd be nice.' So he said, 'Is that for two?' And I was just going to say, 'No, coffee,' when Rebecca said, 'Have a drink'. So I had a drink – £15, mind you: that nearly gave me a headache! It started from there. I had a drink socially with Rebecca on our honeymoon and I still wasn't sure how she felt about that. But she said, 'No, you've changed.' I am now able to drink because I enjoy the drink, not to ease the pain of conflict or because I am angry about something.

Lots of other things begin to change when you let go of your anger and its pain. I was quite aggressive towards people, and one of the most amazing things that happened to me was that I decided I needed to stop the aggression. I was on the golf course and I hit my golf ball into the rough, where other people were. A man in another group hit my golf ball, and I knew he'd hit it, so I approached him. I knew him; he was a local publican. He said, 'No, I haven't,' and I said, 'Well, your ball's over there,' and so it carried on. In the end I could have run over, found my ball, proved him wrong and called him a cheat. But I just said, 'I'll give you one more opportunity – have you hit my ball?' 'No.' So I said to him, 'Then I'm going to honour you here and if you say you didn't, I believe you, thank you.' That was it, and I went off.

The next day I was sitting in my lounge when he came to the front door, came in, and was nearly in tears. I said, 'What's up?' He replied, 'I haven't been able to sleep all night. I don't know what's going on. I've had to phone the golf club, who phoned a local publican who knew you, to find out where you live, Steve.' He said, 'Please forgive me, Steve,' and gave me half a dozen brand new golf balls! Then he said, 'I did hit your ball and I kept it. I haven't been able to sleep all night. I just want you to forgive me.'

That was so big for me: wow, it works. Normally I would have wanted to prove him wrong; I would have wanted to get my revenge. I would have wanted him to feel bad, but in actual fact I allowed him the opportunity for his conscience to react to his guilt. He got it with both barrels. It was amazing and I did nothing: I just said OK, if you say that's true, and the next thing I knew . . . there he was. It's a strange way: that you give to receive. I just gave him that.

The children now are never scared of me. They actually give me 'back chat', which for me is great. They call me the 'ole grey one' and that means they're not scared of me. That means so much. The first time I thought, that's a bit cheeky, but Rebecca said, 'But they're not scared of you, they love you,' and Alistair even came up and said, 'You're so much nicer sober.'

I believe that when people are pushed to the limit they look for inspiration, for something divine, and it's there if they want it. But I think that sometimes you just need to get to the depths. And for me to talk like this now, I mean, it's just amazing. But I had to go through all sorts of processes, kicking and screaming. The bottom line is choice, you know, if you want to be saved. And I was saved, there's no doubt about it.

I now find that where I used to hide being a Christian and being part of Christ Church, I don't need to. We have a float in the big summer carnival. It's a bus with the band on top. I never do the carnival bus. I've always stayed away, but this year I've done it, because this year I can. You hear people, you get the whispers: 'Oh yeah, that's Steve, he's a bit, you know, going to church. Oh, he's a Christian – born again!' This will be my declaration that, 'Hey, you don't have to whisper about it, I'm here.'

So for me it's quite big, you know, because it's my home town. But I look back to all the past and I don't want to go there any more. This is my choice, which is life. That's it!

For me, if it wasn't for Christ Church, the community and God, Rebecca and I wouldn't be here now with a lovely family. She's got a good job, I've got a good job, but I know where I want to go now. I've got to redeem what I lost. Academically I've already started to. I'm just finishing a Diploma in Management with Management Training International (MTI) and the Chartered Management Institute. I really want to redeem something because I'm very good at organizing. I love organizing. I want to start leading, managing in some way, teaching maybe. I see myself possibly in golf as well, to redeem something that was lost many, many years ago. So I see it as a bright future. I find it absolutely exciting, because compared with where I was five years ago, even a couple of years ago, where I'm looking now is fantastic to me. I've got a renewed impetus: I'm really looking forward to it. And I can drink socially, I can drink in moderation. The addiction has gone, because the history's been dealt with. It's as if it never happened.[2]

Life After Debt
James and Christa Allen

James: I am 42, and have lived in Deal since 1972. After being a chorister as a child I left church altogether until Christa joined Christ Church. I'm about to join a project team with my employer, delivering training overseas, and I love cricket, fishing and playing the saxophone.

Christa: I'm 38. James and I have been married for thirteen years and we have two children, Jessica (2) and Megan (6 months). I've been in Deal since I was 9 and joined Christ Church when it started. I went on the first ever workshop. I've just completed an Access to Higher Education course in Music.

Five years. Sometimes it feels like, 'Has it really been that long?' Sometimes it feels more like, 'Is that all?'

The last five years have taken us from being two very separate individual people, married in name but virtually divorced in terms of actual physical contact or relationship, living in a bungalow that didn't suit us and wasn't really us, two very unhappy people, to the place where we're now working at being married, and actually confident of the fact that we are husband and wife, nothing else but husband and wife. Even to the point where we actually think of each other as lovers. We're working at being a family and all that that actually means, nurturing two beautiful children. It's been the work of the Lord, and we're still not sure how He did it.

At the beginning of those five years, being in debt was just the way we lived. It wasn't the reason why either of us began our journey, but it was the thing that stopped us in our tracks and shocked us into choosing to believe there was another way. For that to happen we had to be willing to change, and then we had to be willing to trust the Lord.

Although our childhoods were different in a lot of ways, both of us suffered a lack of affirmation from our families, and in the end that showed up in the way we handled money. We never actually learnt how to build up the other person. We missed it, but didn't know how to do it. We didn't really know how to do relationship, how to give each other emotional support, how to ask for it. There was that non-connecting between us. So we bought things. The way we affirmed each other was to buy what we wanted. The only way we could show affection was to buy something for someone. So we would go out and buy the biggest, the most expensive thing.

James: The best you could get – that was my focus. Christa and I bought things for each other and we bought things for ourselves. I suppose we were making up for the way it had been for us as children. I got presents as a child but they were never quite right. At Christmas or for my birthday I would always ask for a specific present, and my parents would buy the nearest they could to what I wanted. It was always the nearest. So in later life I would say to myself, 'OK, stuff everybody else. I will go out and buy what I want.'

Was 'near enough is good enough' all I was worth to them? And then, because I needed to do that, I hurt Christa. Instead of saying to her, 'I'd like this,' and allowing her to fail, it would be, 'I'm not giving you any option to do that – I am going to go and buy what I want.' This gave her no scope in any way to do what she could, gave her no chance to learn about what I liked, or why, or where I was coming from.

Christa: From my angle it began in a home situation where my father was on the dole, and spent most of that on drink, and my mother lived in debt. That was the example, the upbringing I had. But the real problem was at school. My secondary school was a convent, a private school. There were kids there who on their seventeenth birthday would pass you on the way to the station, offering you a lift in their brand new car. Some of them got taken to school in Rolls-Royces. There were some very, very rich kids.

I wouldn't say I was ever bullied in the sense of being physically harmed, but emotionally, verbally, I was abused every single day, because my dad was on the dole. I had two best friends whose fathers were a company director and a bank manager, and my dad was on the dole. 'Oh, your dad's nothing. You don't have any money, you don't have anything. You don't have clothes to wear.' On and on. That, for me, was what I was fighting against, I believe. And then when I was working and earning, I said, 'Oh, I've got money,' but I hadn't. Not enough to make the difference. I just had to get it from some source – any way I could. I brought my mother's history into the marriage. She was bad with money and so was I.

James: Although I had had this very strict, very good training where spending was concerned – 'If you haven't got the money in the bank, you don't buy it' – I still joined in because of all my baggage. We just collected credit cards, lots and lots of credit cards.

Peter and Susan teach that you can say, 'Lord, what a mess! Please help!' And He will. But only when you stop thinking that you can cope, when you are willing to let go of the fear and the pride and the history.

We thought we could cope. One lucky break and everything would be back under control. We could cope with it. We got to the point where we would sit down in front of the television on a Saturday evening, when we'd spent £10 to £15 on the lottery, waiting for the numbered balls to come down. This week, this week . . .

Christa: We were each on a journey, doing homework, but we weren't doing it about the debt. We were doing the journey separately. Part of that time we were actually living apart. I had been doing it for about a year, I think, when I did a major piece of homework in relation to my mother and suddenly woke up to the realization that for the first time, at 36, I wanted children. That's when it all came to a stop.

Our past was not only stealing our present, through the debt (among other issues); it was now threatening our future as well. It was threatening my chance of having children, my being able to leave work to look after them, our having a house where we could bring them up.

We had to get out of the fix we were in. It looked like an absolute impossibility, but we had to start somewhere. We began to repent, saying sorry to the Lord and to ourselves. That was the first thing I had to do, to say sorry for the mess I was in, and grieve for the position I was in. That was the first shock for me. We actually had to invite the Lord into it, to redeem, and even though at that time we thought there was no hope of ever getting out of it, we had to give Him the opportunity to redeem this mess that we'd made, otherwise the future's . . . what future? I wanted a life, but we'd screwed up too badly. We had to ask the Lord to intervene and redeem.

James: For me, the worst was going to Peter, someone I respected, loved really, not a father figure exactly but a sort of dad, and say, 'Look, this is actually where we are. This is what we've done.' That was the lowest point. It was so humiliating.

After that, once I'd actually said, 'This is where we are,' once I'd done the telling, the rest was just a kick into gear. Let's get on with this, because this has got to be sorted. Just get on and do it: make the plan, get the scissors out. Once the standing orders were in place and the cards were cut up, that was it. And in January 2002, shortly after Christa moved back in, as part of submitting to the Lord, we made a declaration: we wanted to be in a position where 'I, James, can earn enough money in a job that I am happy in to support both of us, so that Christa can explore the possibility of being a wife and mother. We would like to do this in a new home. And where I, James, have enough spare money to be involved in a new boat.' We were declaring we had faith in a God who could do something bigger than just help us survive. There would be life after debt. It was our 'mission statement'.

So as part of the scenario of working to get the debt paid off, we decided to put our bungalow on the market, having realized that it was totally wrong for us. We had a huge garden we weren't interested in, in a street full of not just retired but really elderly people. My mum's a keen gardener, Dad's an allotment man and Mum always wanted a bungalow. It had been bought at my parents' suggestion, and we hadn't looked beyond that. And it was a retirement bungalow. We'd already given up our life and retired. We were not yet 40 and we were living in our deathbed. We said goodbye to it, prayed and even said sorry to it, too. We let it go.

Changed Lives

The house we are living in now is one I'd driven past several years before and thought, 'I'd love to live there one of these days.' It was on the market, but at a very high price. We'd shopped around and the maximum mortgage we could get was £155,000. So I told the estate agent that if I could have it for £155,000, I'd buy it. He said, 'Oh no, they wouldn't accept that.' But they did.

It was completely unreal: this just doesn't happen. Then the day we exchanged contracts on the house, the sale fell through on the bungalow. It looked as though everything was falling apart. I gave the estate agent fourteen days to find us a buyer and nothing appeared. But then the estate agent selling the house to us said he'd sell it. We went to the Lord: Help! Within a week, the estate agent came to us and offered to buy it for cash.

So somehow we'd gone from a retirement bungalow to a massive four-bedroom detached house with room for kids, family and everything else. And, as Christa says, we can have people staying from the community.

Christa: We moved in December, and the following February I got pregnant! Which is another part of the story.

James: At Christmas 1980 I had a major motorbike crash, and I was told by my doctor that because of the accident, I probably wouldn't be able to have kids. I didn't want kids turning out like me anyway, and Christa had had the same feeling on that. But when we moved, it was, 'OK, next step.' We'd got the house as part of our 'mission statement' and now I had to give Christa the chance to explore the idea of being a wife and mother. We basically said to the Lord, 'We give you permission to meddle with us,' and three months later Christa was pregnant. A huge pile of homework went into that one, because it went against twenty years of believing a lie that said I couldn't do this, I couldn't have this.

Jessica was born just a week before my birthday: there she was, and I just cried. So we had Christa on maternity leave, money coming in, house and child.

Christa: I went back to work part-time, which was not the ideal. The ideal would have been not to go back at all. But two years ago we cleared the last debt completely, and that was amazing. That was when James stood up and told the whole church I didn't have to work any more. I could stop working now when the next one came along. And here she is, six months old.

People ask me how it's happened and I tell them I don't know. I do not know how that worked. All I know is it happened. We were in a little house, up to our eyeballs in debt, no money for anything, then we moved to a very big house and we've got more money and two children.

James: Christa and I both stood up and told our church family, a hundred people, how it was. And that's where we're at now. The way the mortgage rates are moving, it's getting tight, so I need the next promotion, an influx of money or a new job. Some of that is about asking the Lord to redeem twenty-five years of 'groveller's work'. Having believed I was a failure, I want to prove that actually there is quite a remarkable brain in my head, capable of learning, explaining, putting things on paper. In 2002 I did a psychometric test, to help explore my future.[3] I thought there would be one little black line showing what I could do, but it was virtually black all the way across: 'You can do whatever you want.' But it was heavily geared towards lecturing and teaching.

In the present climate, if you want to get career advancement over 40 there is so much that needs to happen. But because of all the homework I've done, there's nothing standing in its way now, or not much. No more 'I don't deserve it,' 'I can't have it,' or 'I shouldn't have it.'

Christa: James and I are aware of the pitfalls. We could very, very easily blow ourselves up again. And we just have to be really careful not to do that. We are able to make the right choices now, but only if we're standing with the Lord and we're going onwards with our journeys, working on it. If we're not faithful to that, we could get into disaster very easily.

God's been great and He is still redeeming. The children, the house, our work as well, what's coming up for James . . . God's still in the middle of doing it.

Ferris Wheels and Weighing Scales
Yvonne Harrison

I'm 33 and single. I've been in Deal for five years but was born in North Yorkshire. I committed my life to the Lord when I was 5. I started my Psychology degree at Bangor University and finished it at the University of Canterbury. I love working with children and want to see Rapha translated for children. I also enjoy teaching at Rapha workshops and am in the middle of training to teach adults.

This is about addiction. So, what does the word 'addiction' mean in the language of my experience? The way I see it, addiction consists of a set of behaviours that I can no longer control or change, whereas a habit is something I have the ability to change. It's when you don't know you've done it till it's too late and you're wishing you hadn't – again.

I have done lots of things that look like what most people think of as addiction, and still do some of them on a bad day, but underlying all of that was the real issue: I was addicted to self-hate. I have learnt about this here in the Christ Church community. And I have learnt what to do about it in order to be healed, so that I needn't expect to be spending time in mental hospitals on and off for the rest of my life.

I got sick and was in a mental hospital quite a few

times in my teens, and the last time, while I was at university in Bangor, I decided that I needed to go somewhere where I wasn't getting more and more sick. It didn't matter how long it took, or how hard the journey was. I needed some hope and I needed healing, because the people round me were saying, 'Every two years you're going to be in a mental hospital for about three or four weeks,' and I didn't want that.

So I phoned Susan and said, 'I know you do workshops, but actually I think I'm going to need a little bit more long-term help than that: is there anything you can offer me? I need some help, I'm ready to give up, and it's either I get some help or I die – end of story – I can't do this any more.' Susan said, 'We'll help you and make it as if it never happened, as long as you're prepared to take personal responsibility for what's happened to you.' She promised to send me an 'introductory tape', to help me decide. I listened to this simple presentation about the workshops and on it was a moment when Susan asked Noella, a member of the community, to speak about her journey of healing. There was a long silence and then Noella said, 'Help me out here, Susan. How bad was it? I can't remember.' And I just thought, '*Oh my God – if it can be like that for her, then actually it can be like that for me.*'

With every last breath of tenacity within me, I focused on coming to Deal to start this journey. 'I'm going to do this. This is just like passing an exam! I'm going to do this. I'm not going to let go, and I'm going to make it work.' So I arrived in Deal and Susan said, 'Right, have a holiday for two weeks.' After that I went on a workshop. I wasn't absorbing the teaching, but I sat through it and I still wanted to stay. This was the first time they'd actually had someone out of mental hospital and brought them straight into the community.

I would compare self-hate to a Ferris wheel. A Ferris

wheel has baskets on it. Now for me these baskets have been filled with things like smoking, drinking, food and binge spending, and they just go round and round. As they come down they empty out, and then you get rid of one, but you've got all these other baskets still full. So I've spent my life hopping from one addiction to the other, all the way round. You deal with one and then you deal with the next, but they're perpetuating themselves as they're going round. They never actually go, because the Ferris wheel is still there. And while the Ferris wheel is still there and the baskets are still there, the baskets keep filling up again.

I believe, out of my own experience, that no one will ever crack their addiction to smoking, drinking or anything else until they've got rid of the wheel. You can see the baskets, because they're there. You know what they are, but the Ferris wheel that carries them you can't see. But you can get to be able to see it and you can deal with it.

I've been on the journey for around four-and-a-half years. So I've had a little bit of practice at recognizing when I'm about to slip into my Ferris wheel, which is my self-hate. I'll describe a typical situation. Remember as you read it that all of this is unconscious.

Suppose I'm at church on a Sunday morning: I go up to Susan and ask her how she is, and I ask her for a hug goodbye. And she then says, 'My arms are full of equipment right now,' because she's carrying her stuff to the car.

What I hear from her through my filter of self-hate is, 'I don't want to give you a hug because I don't want you near me, because you carry horrible darkness.' So, then I go home and I get on the Ferris wheel and I decide, 'Oh, I must be a horrible person. Peter and Susan must have been thinking for months now how dark I am on the inside.' So the lie has already come in, and now I'm believing the lie.

In order to describe what happens next I'm going to change the metaphor, but stay with me. When I begin to believe the lies, it's like stepping onto the edge of a staircase. I've committed myself to the next level of going down by believing the lie. So then I look for that lie in my other relationships and I see it everywhere. 'Oh, Roman and Rachael are busy – they don't want to speak to me.' They must have been talking to Peter and Susan and must think I'm horrible. I wonder why I'm horrible – 'God, please show me why I'm so horrible on the inside.'

God stays silent, so therefore God must hate me as well. Why is God choosing not to love me any more? Actually God is staying silent because He's got nothing to say: from His perspective, I'm lovely, so He's not going to answer the question, 'Why am I so horrible?' So it goes down and down until it gets to the bottom, which is, 'Why am I still alive?' And as I get further and further down, my sight becomes tunnelled. I lose the ability to see anything other than my lie. My vision becomes more and more distorted and I can't see beyond the lies any more. It gets darker and darker, and when I get to the bottom, it's as if I've climbed down a huge well and I can't get out. I can't see any perspective other than what I believe to be true, which is based upon lies but feels true for me. 'Well look, that person ignored me, that person's really angry with me, that person isn't speaking to me . . .'

So now I've got to the bottom, believing the lies, hating myself. Well, I'll have a drink to make me feel better about myself. I'll go and spend some money to pull myself out of this pit that I'm in. At least if I look nice on the outside, people won't notice how bad I feel about myself on the inside. I'll have a cigarette to calm myself down because I feel so bad about myself, about what happened before.

I only realize what I've done when I get to the bottom. And then I'll talk to Susan and she will say, 'Why are you listening to your lies?' 'They're not lies, they're truth,' I reply. 'They are lies,' she says.

It doesn't have to get as bad as that if you catch it on the first or second stage, and living in community is a very good way of knowing. In this community, if you look at somebody else and you *think* they hate you, it's a good sign of where you are, particularly if that person has a level of maturity in Christ that means you know instinctively that they don't hate you.

So when did the hating begin and how did my particular Ferris wheel get built?

I was born into a family with a history of mental illness. My mum nearly died during childbirth – so that was 'Yvonne's fault'. Mum was very ill and I had to look after her, so I was very angry as a child because I had all this extra responsibility and I kept getting it wrong – so 'Yvonne is a naughty child.' Mum hated me because I was physically well, because I was quite intelligent, and anything that she could do, I could do almost as well and sometimes better, and because I looked like my dad, her ex-husband who had betrayed her. For me to be a good girl and live in my family, I was required by her and the rest of my family to hate myself.

When I was 12, I was put into a children's home and . . . well, to everyone's surprise they discovered I was normal. 'We were expecting a little monster and what we got was a lost little girl who just wanted to play and hadn't been allowed to.' And they were quite shocked. Back in my mum's house, within two days, once again I couldn't control my temper. I wanted to kill her because of the regime that she had me under, continually to hate myself, continually to live in this dark pit and continually to be her carer and be the adult when actually I was the child. This was just a direct abuse of everything that I should have been given.

Then my mum died. Aged 14 and back in the children's home, I picked up the drinking, because I couldn't get the pain out. That's when I made a pact with hate: that no matter what happened, I would always hate. Hate would be my friend. I would use hate to destroy everybody around me, because they had hated me, and I would make myself powerful through it and nobody would ever be able to touch me like that again. Not just the sexual abuse but the emotional abuse and the spiritual abuse. 'I'm going to be strong now.' But as soon as I'd made hate my friend, it was like signing my own death warrant.

The greatest weapon I had against God, for what I perceived He had done to me, was to kill myself off, because actually He loved me. So the only way for me to get back at Him was to hate myself. I gave the keys to my heart over to hate and she took them. And I didn't know any better.

By the time I arrived at Christ Church I'd forgotten those decisions. My first awareness came when Peter and Susan had a session with me in the July that I arrived and Peter told me how much I hated myself. That was quite shocking. I'd forgotten the decisions I'd made. I was just living in self-hate as a daily reality. So Peter put it on my agenda, because I was unable to have a relationship with anybody, anybody at all – I couldn't let them near me, because they hated me. Why would I want anybody near me?

First of all I had to start undoing my decision to hate, and see the extent to which I would self-harm. I couldn't keep a job, because I'd be late or I'd do something that would get me the sack, so then I could hate myself. I would pull my hair out, so that I'd have some pain, then I could hate myself more. Everything I did was a function, a feeding, of self-hate. I had to realize what I was doing to myself on a daily basis and to see that ultimately this was going to kill me. At the core of it was a choice, literally, between 'life' and 'death', and that translated into a choice between love and hate. So that was the initial decision. But that wasn't enough. I've had to say sorry for every decision I'd made to hate myself, to feel the pain of that decision and then undo it and put something better in its place.

So now I get up in the morning and I give myself enough time to get dressed and have something to eat and then go to work, rather than leaving everything to the last minute, rushing out of the house and then getting to work in a fluster. That is part of me loving myself, choosing to love myself. And if I'm going to choose to love then I'm going to choose to do the washing up, so I don't have to do it when it gets too much and the kitchen looks horrible.

Eventually – and I'm almost there now – you come to a point where the Ferris wheel is still operating, but there isn't a motor any more. It's a matter of knowing that actually I don't have to live like this any more. I don't need the wheel, and the more I focus on what I want to have in its place, the less the wheel exists. It's as if it's fading into nothingness, because the less attention you give the wheel, the less you need to worry about it. And the more you focus on the love, the less you need the hate. It's not that suddenly God goes and kicks it over so it's not there any more. Rather, it fades.

I now think that the more you put good habits in place of bad ones, the more you choose to love yourself and the more you choose to love other people, the less chance you have of going back into the hate. And where you start is with an act of will: 'I have to do this, just because I have to.' It is literally as cold and as calculated as that. 'I choose to forgive myself and welcome God's forgiveness.' In the beginning I did it on the hour, every hour, and people have said to me, 'You can't. That's not feasible, that's not realistic.' But if you really, really, want to change, if you really, really can't live the old way any more, it is.

I had a little card in my handbag that said, 'I choose to love myself,' four times over. On the hour, every hour, I said, 'Lord I'm so sorry that I've messed up again,' and forgave myself. I did that for about a year and it was like tipping a set of weighing scales. The more times I said, 'Forgive myself, choose to love,' even though it was cognitive and I was doing it in my head, using my will, and not spontaneously from my spirit, one side of the weighing scales was going up. Finally I reached what Peter calls a 'tipping point'. As soon as I'd put enough into the love/forgive side to tip the scales, God could show me why I hated myself so much. He could show me how my Ferris wheel got built.

So now I had to deal with my mother. I had to see why she'd done what she'd done and choose not to come under her influence any more. I had to say sorry for all the decisions that I'd made in order for me to hate myself, and take the sting, the power out of it. So I started along that journey, to take the power out of what she'd said, each time choosing God's perspective instead of my mother's.

I had to deal with each thing that happened. OK, my mum hated me because I wasn't this, didn't look like that, or looked like my dad. I had to ask God to take it away. I would give Him the pain of what my mother had said to me and let it go, asking God to forgive her, then choose to stand under Christ and choose His identity for me and not hers. With every bit of the hate, the anger, the revenge, it was to choose what God is going to say rather than what I am going to say. Eventually I was able just to let the hate go and pick up the love. I was quite sick: carrying that amount of hate would kill anybody off, but every time I've dealt with an issue, I've picked up a bit more life.

When I was 5, I met Jesus. He promised me that it was going to be OK. It's so great He did, because actually what happened after that was the systematic annihilation of who I was. I think something inside me always knew that actually even though it was dire, God was there. Even so, I'd reached the point of giving up when I got here. And I remember quite clearly that I wanted to put my head in the oven, in the June of my arriving, and Susan was very cross: 'Well, you've taken yourself out of our care.' And I said, 'What?' 'By threatening to kill yourself you've taken yourself out of our care.' 'But I don't want to.' Then she said, 'You'd better go now, sit with Jesus and tell Him you're sorry, and start dismantling this now, because you can't do this any more – you're abusing others by your abuse of yourself.'

When I got on my knees and said sorry to God, He showed me a picture. A bunch of skeletons were dancing around a pool and they were all the people from my past. I was in the middle and my flesh had been stripped. I had to ask Christ in, and He put me on a stretcher and carried me out. He wrapped my bones, because that's all that was left, in bandages. He carried me into the house where Peter and Susan see people and left me there. And He said, 'You just need to let yourself recover now.' And that was the first choice I had to make. It was an active choice, to leave all that behind and then to start to dismantle everything I'd done to myself, to recognize the Ferris wheel of my self-hate, deal with it and then watch it fade.

Some Comments

We talk in CCD and *Rapha* about the 'empty chair'. We invite people to imagine that the person who has most hurt them is sitting on an empty chair in the middle of the room. We then suggest they talk to that person, telling them how they really feel about what has happened. Most people feel silly doing this to begin with, but in time they overcome their embarrassment and fear and can start. We suggest that as they engage the pain they give it to the Lord: 'Lord, I do not want this any more!' Using this approach, rather than meeting the person face to face, has several benefits. It does not matter that the abuser may now be dead, and there is no risk that the abuse might be repeated if they were to meet them again.

Most addictions will be 'driven' by deeper issues, e.g. James's and Christa's family history of poverty, Steve's revenge against his mum, Yvonne's self-hate. Most people think they are choosing of their own free will to be addicted. They have to learn that there will be deeper reasons. To be truly free of most addictions it is helpful to deal first with these deeper drives.

For instance, the model we use for tackling substance addictions is a three-level one, with a superficial biochemical aspect on the surface, a social level below this (e.g. 'all my friends do it as well'), and an emotional aspect at the root (e.g. 'I love the intoxicating hate'). Much of the time it is the emotional attachment that has to be owned and removed by the person. We see little point in temporarily breaking the biochemical aspects of the addiction until the emotional drive or attachment is dealt with, since the person will merely return to the habit. Once the drive has been undone, it is much easier to let go of the addiction. For instance, Steve had to deal with his revenge against his mother, Yvonne had to own and want to let go of her self-hate.

As children grow up, we are often shocked to hear them shout out, 'I hate you!' A toxic self-hate and self-harm normally walk together. If we hate our body, for instance, we will allow ourselves and others to harm it with addictions, or a lifestyle that treats it with contempt, e.g. sleeping around, overeating, etc. Our unrighteous hate steals our perspective on what we are doing, so we can do it all the more. So, as we begin to see what we are doing and own up to our chosen blindness, we will feel the need to forgive ourselves. God has already forgiven us, but we need to forgive ourselves. Yet we cannot do this until we have begun to see the extent of our self-harm. Beginning to own this is always a major step for anyone on the journey.

You may have noticed Yvonne's threat to kill herself. When people who have a history of self-harm join our community, we make it clear to them that if they threaten or attempt to take their own life, we are obliged to take them straight down to the Accident & Emergency department of the local hospital, or hand them over to the local mental health team. Attempting to kill oneself in the community automatically excludes a person from the community. We follow this policy for several reasons, but chiefly we see such threats of self-harm as abuse against the whole community, as well as an assault against the people they are staying with. Also, we are not equipped long-term for the full-time cover that such people need.

Notes

[1] One of the regular practices we have in the congregation is that members of the community share a story of an area of change they have recently experienced. Sometimes, like

Steve, they want to say sorry as a public declaration, although we only encourage this when the fruit of the change is already clearly visible.

2 This is a common phrase in our work. Although the memory of the damage will still be there, the actual pain, the habits, the drives are all gone. The emotion keeps the painful memories alive, so when you give the pain to the Lord, the memories can fade.

3 As part of the personal redemption of an individual's life we frequently have them do psychometric tests that help clarify for them what their natural skill set is, that is, what they are naturally talented at doing. Everyone is good at something. When a person subsequently moves in these areas of natural ability, it means they will excel academically and practically if they apply themselves.

7

Loss

Loss is such a common thing. We all lose things. We've all lost someone we love, a favourite job, a friend who has moved away, or even our health. Perhaps loss has come through divorce (our own or others'), or it's the loss of a hope or dream which can no longer be fulfilled. We started the book with Kate's story, talking of how Jesus took away the pain of her lost child. So we finish with two stories of early loss.

We could have chosen two examples of uncomplicated loss. But these stories you are about to read have loss intertwined with many other layers of damage. Christine's twin died when he was in the womb. Until the Lord healed her, that loss fundamentally affected who she became. Mike – well, he will tell you that he lost himself.

Goodbye, My Twin
Christine Marsh

I'm 57 and have recently married Fred. I have a daughter and son from my first marriage and two grandchildren. I was born in Leicester and moved to Deal when I was 16. I still love living here. I joined Christ Church at the beginning, having been a Christian since 1982. My hobbies are swimming and taking my dog Cracker for walks, and I love meeting people.

I started going to Peter for help after my first husband and I split up, but this story isn't about that. It's about another loss, one that happened before I was even born. I didn't admit this to myself until I was in my fifties, even though it had affected the whole of my life. It's a story about seeing myself robbed and seeing myself restored, about undoing all the harm, and finally letting the loss happen so that God could redeem it. It's a story of loss and hope.

When my husband left I was devastated. 'You have to make this right,' people said. 'You're a Christian. Reconcile.' At that stage I wanted to, but my husband had moved out. There was lots of advice, but not much help. I had no sense of God being there, but I felt guilty if I said He wasn't. I was a Christian, so I thought I should be able to cope with anything. I was trying to protect God, pretending I was all right. I thought that people wouldn't like God if I said I wasn't all right.

'You haven't grieved,' the counsellors said. 'You haven't even got angry.' I was in denial of my feelings in order to survive, for the children's sake. I wanted them to think everything was all right. I knew I hadn't grieved. I know it sounds obvious, that you cry, but I had never cried. And anger? I had always felt it was wrong to get angry as a Christian. And my father was quite an angry man; he was quite fiery. So I was always frightened of getting angry. It was all such a strain.

I really thought my life had finished. I was in my little house and I had everything nearby. I was just existing. I couldn't keep a job and I never would see anyone. I thought I was quite good just to be able to cope after my husband left.

It was before Christ Church started, and Peter and Mary Holmes, Susan and some of the others were at the time all members of the church that I belonged to. One Sunday I went forward for prayer for my back. I'd been doing care work, as well as cleaning, and I'd hurt my back. I was sitting at the front and I knew that the minister wasn't going to come over. There were a lot of people, but I felt that someone else was going to speak to me. Now Peter didn't actually go up and pray with people, not up to the front there. He just came and sat next to me and I instantly started crying, which was so unlike me. 'I've come forward for prayer,' I said, 'for my back. But I don't think that's it.' And I cried. He just said, 'Well, if there's anything I can do, if you'd like to drop in anytime for a cup of tea and a chat, you must feel free. I'll leave it with you.'

And from that moment, I thought, 'There's hope.' Up until then no one had ever said, 'There is hope,' or, 'I think I can help you.' It was always, 'You've got to do this,' or 'You haven't done that,' all of it too hard, all of it adding to my guilt.

I didn't know much about Peter's ministry except for the change I had seen in a very close friend of mine. I felt it was real. I could see there was a difference in her that I'd never seen before, and I had known her for about fifteen years. Recently she had begun to ring me up and tell me she was seeing Peter and was doing homework, and I was so sceptical about it all, but seeing her I thought there must be something in it. We used to walk along the seafront, the two of us with Cracker, my dog, and she used to tell me all these things.

So, that afternoon, I rang Peter and we had an introductory meeting, a chat about how physical problems could often be helped by looking for their root in an emotional or spiritual problem. Everything he said gave me hope. If I wanted to go and have another chat I could, but first I must go away and think about what he had said.

The second time I went to see him, my first real session, Peter explained that this would be a journey and I would be spending time asking the Holy Spirit to show me areas of my life that he would like to deal with. I knew a little bit about that from my friend, so it was really a question of whether I was going to go for it or not. I had nothing to lose, because I didn't have any other hope. So I went back.

This time Peter chatted about areas of my past, my mother and all sorts of other things I thought were irrelevant to what I had really come about, which was the loss of my husband. He explained that as people deal with areas from their past, including the time before they were born, and as they clear those out of the way, it is easier to deal with the more recent things.[1] I was very mixed up about it all, and very sceptical, but thought I might as well try it.

Peter sent me home with a list of six points, so I could

ask the Holy Spirit, ask the Lord, to show me which was the 'hottest' (his expression). In other words, which one was affecting me the most. I really thought, at that stage, it wasn't going to work, because I didn't think of myself as a very 'feeling' person. But I was learning that if I were willing to be open to the Holy Spirit He would begin to show me the issues in my spirit that He wanted to heal.

I started to recall incidents from my childhood. A favourite game when I was a child was to put a black scarf over my head, over my blond hair, and pretend there were two of us: one fair and one dark. Only it wasn't a game. I used to pretend that we talked to each other. I remembered how often I had felt I was a misfit, lonely, alone, sometimes wondering if I was a twin, perhaps even a Siamese twin (conjoined, they would say now).

I recalled getting the idea as a child that if I received special treatment because I was 'the only one', as the adults said, this must be because it was a huge disadvantage to be the only one. So normality must be more than one.

Then a shock. I remembered a conversation my dad and I had while we were playing cards, when he just threw in the fact that I should have been one of twins. But because there wasn't enough food for him in the womb, this twin, this brother I should have had, that I had known nothing about, had died. At the age that I discovered this I must have already learnt to push pain down and pretend to be unconcerned, because nothing happened. No questions were asked. He told me I must never talk about it with my mum, as she would get upset. My father's favourite saying was 'Subject closed' whenever we were talking about anything confrontational, emotional or debatable. So there was little chance of bringing the subject up again.

Another thing that came back to me was that my mother was very angry after I was born, and I was made to feel guilty for causing her pain.

I began to have dreams, a series of very distressing dreams.[2] In my first dream I was a baby, but I turned into a doll, and then I was a child and I was given the job of seeing if I could soften the doll by getting close to her. As I got close to the doll, she warmed to me and changed into a beautiful baby. My parents were in a prison-like building far away. I felt they were angry and hated me, and my mother was frightened I'd ask questions. Mum hated me and Dad followed. I tried to escape over a high security wall with broken glass on the top, and then, as I looked over, I saw my dead twin, a boy, on the ground, and I managed to escape and ran into a stranger's arms. I realized that this dream contained a specific revelation of truth for my journey, on which the Lord and I were going to have to travel together.

I knew I was going to unpack it, I needed to unpack it, and I knew I needed time because it was so upsetting. There were lots of things upsetting about it. One was the hate from my mother. I could see the dream, it was so clear, and even though I was far enough on in my journey to have already looked into the issue of my mother, and the things she'd carried and I'd felt, this was still horrible to look at. It was still very painful. So this was the journey.

Over the next few weeks I found myself remembering how much my mother hated babies, especially boys – she always told me she was very frightened of children and babies, and didn't really like or enjoy being a mother. She never liked the responsibility of being a parent. She just hated being a woman, hated her womanhood, and always felt ashamed.

Then I had another dream, and the dream included the words that my mother was involved in child sacrifice. I didn't know whether it was years ago, I didn't know whether it meant that she went to a coven somewhere. I didn't know a thing. It was just a wild, most peculiar feeling I had once I heard these words, but I had made a decision not to dismiss anything, and I knew there had been occult practices in my mother's family.

She and my grandma, her mother, were always interested in occult things, so that is an area I had grown up with. There were things my mother and I were into: the spiritualist church, ouija boards, fortune-telling, which my mother taught me. I had always been dragged along to watch, from when I was quite young, but I hated it. I always felt oppressed by it. But it was normal in my mother's family. I'd repented of this when I first became a Christian, but now I realized there must be debris remaining.

I can always remember my mother not liking children, and I remember her hating having children round. She'd always said, as I'd got older, 'Oh, it's so funny that you like children because I don't.' Or she'd say, 'Thank goodness I didn't have a boy!' It didn't seem odd at the time, because that's just how she was, but a sort of picture was becoming more and more clear. I felt there was something she had inherited, that had come down through the families, to make her have this hate towards boys.[3] That's how I felt it. A hate towards babies, not a love that God had instilled in her. So I started to go back to things like the anger in the hospital after I was born. If what I remembered my father saying was true, and if my mother hated babies, especially boys, what had actually happened to my twin? I had desperate questions to ask.

Peter had said to me, when I saw him about all these things, 'What the Lord is doing is giving you a postcard, and he's writing something on it. Then you're getting another. At this stage don't worry about "What does this mean?" (I was going off to the library and looking at books.) Just let it happen; it will all fall into place, and in the end you'll understand.' So this was how it was, until the picture came together.

And now was the time for the Lord to show me further damage in my family's line, and the root it came from. As I felt the sin and saw the evil, I repented of it on behalf of my family, and also for my own sake.

Feeling distraught, and grieving for my twin, I had yet another dream where I felt such a cold, angry hatred towards me. I could see my mother looking at me with such hate, and she was looking at my twin also, with a harmful intent towards him. This was just so clear. It didn't really make sense, but I knew, because it was so clear, that she really did hate him.

Meanwhile, I was growing in my understanding of how we communicate on an emotional and spiritual level, without ever knowing we are. So I could accept that I might not have known about my mother's hatred, but it would still have affected me. Also, that in some way I could have carried this hate into the core of my being. And I had also given it to my children.

As I saw the truth, my anger towards my mother grew stronger. I decided to do some homework on this, pretending she was here to speak to, putting her on the empty chair, expressing my anger and then giving my words and my feelings to the Lord.

Over a period of time my body started telling me what was happening emotionally and spiritually. My fingers were slowly bending over and were terribly painful. Driving, cooking, picking things up became impossible. When asked to help in the kitchen at a *Rapha* workshop, I couldn't, because the pain was so severe. Carrying was absolutely impossible. So what was I carrying?

Mary suggested I asked the Lord. Peter and Susan saw me. Peter told me he had a picture of me holding my twin in my arms in the womb and the body was decomposing and rotting my own flesh. So horrific: could it be true?

I began to learn I was still carrying him, even though he was dead. It was as if, somehow, I could give him some life by doing that. I began to see I was carrying the guilt of killing him, then of playing down my own life so it wouldn't feel so upsetting, that I'd somehow feel less guilty. I was 'carrying death'. Over the years this had built up, and now my hands were suffering as I continued to try to hold on to him.

It was a struggle to realize I wasn't responsible for his death, and couldn't continue to protect him. I was living vicariously, thinking that if I were happy it would emphasize his living sadness and pain. I said sorry to the Lord for the sin that caused me to live, in order to stop my brother dying.

I forget now the extent of how awful it was, because it's gone. I struggle to remember the extent of it. The whole of my life I'd been this person, because of feeling I was the guilty one, somehow trying to make it right, just wanting to 'do' something to make it right, and in doing that I'd robbed myself of who I should have been. I took it through my childhood; I took it into my marriage. I never really knew why I was the way I was, why I never felt I could show any joy or excitement.

So now I knew I had to give my twin to the Lord, that I couldn't carry him. I knew I had to give him to the Lord, that He had created him anyway and was his maker. But then I found myself doubting, with all that had been going on in my family. I realized I didn't believe that God was powerful enough to protect him from the Enemy's claims.

I gave him to the Lord, but I didn't know whether the Lord could take him. That went on for quite a few weeks. I was giving him to the Lord and in my head I knew that He had created him and he had gone to be with Him, but

I couldn't feel it. Then I had to get it into my head that I wasn't guilty, that I hadn't killed my twin. I had to renounce this lie.

My hands got a little bit better, but they still weren't quite right, so I felt there was still something else. Then I was asked by somebody, 'What else could you be doing with your hands?' and I said, 'I just feel like wringing my mother's neck!' That's how I was feeling, because of all the things that had happened and all that I had felt. I wanted to wring my mother's neck. Could I have ever said such a thing? It became evident I was punishing myself, out of revenge, and believed that by punishing myself I would somehow be hurting my mother.

I felt justice hadn't been done. Also I was angry with myself and wouldn't forgive myself for allowing her to get away with it. I struggled, but couldn't let go of the revenge to begin with. It was clear I was still very angry with my mother, so I dealt with all that. I declared I didn't want to live that way any more. I gave her to the Lord, and that was another whole story. I didn't find it easy to actually get angry, so I really needed help till I had got rid of all my anger towards her.

Then I had to realize that I was blaming myself, so there was part of me that still wouldn't give my twin to the Lord. There was part of me that was still feeling that somewhere along the line, 'justice must be done'.

So this wasn't getting better, or maybe only slightly. And I felt I was just bashing against all these things. Eventually I decided one morning just to leave the house and go off somewhere and talk to the Lord.

I went to the beach. It was very, very early (I had never got up early before – I never do that normally) and I was crying out to the Lord about all this. I had been crying and crying for weeks about the loss of my twin. That had started when I began looking at this issue. But now I was wanting to give him to the Lord and not carry him. I looked up at the sky, where the sun was behind the clouds, and I thought, 'I have to *do* something here, to *do* it. So I'm just going to look up to you, Lord, and look at the sky.' And I said goodbye to him: 'There you are, Lord, you can take my twin. I say goodbye.'

As I looked at the clouds I saw a picture of a baby. You know how the clouds are with the sun, moving all the while. It was as I said, 'I give him to you, Lord,' that I saw the baby. Then I saw a picture of a man who I felt would be my twin now: that's my twin . . . He put his hand out, gliding through the sky, and I was wondering where he was going. Then I saw an amazing picture of what I felt was the Lord, who came up to the man and carried him. Then the whole picture disappeared, the sun came out and an enormous peace came over me. I knew in my heart that my twin was now with his Father.

I felt I was no longer tied to him. I was now free from the pain, the guilt I had carried for so long. Finally, I had let go of my twin. God was carrying him now. Gradually, little by little, my hands straightened out, the pain subsided. Now, at last, I was free to grow into the person He had created me to be. Isn't God amazing?

Finding Mike, a Story of Loss
Mike Gregory

I am in my early fifties, married to Julie, with four girls, Laura, Hannah, Ruth and Kathleen, aged from 16 to 11. I was born in Surrey, but have been in Deal since 1980, when I came down to join the Marines. I've been at Christ Church since it started but have many years' history in churches. I'd like to set up my own care home in the next few years. I play tennis in a lovely park where family and friends can have picnics.

The loss was the loss of 'me'. Yet it was not that I went away and others experienced the loss. Instead, the person I should have been wasn't there, never had been there.

My earliest memory of loss was wondering where my father was, and eventually finding out that he was living with his girlfriend, and that my only real contact with him was by visiting his girlfriend. Although I didn't know what a normal family was, I had a sense something was not good.

I remember things just hurt, but I didn't understand why. I had this big red plastic boat with a yellow top, and somebody made holes in it so that it filled with water, and that was a loss. Someone bought me a camera for Christmas. It was my present, but I wasn't allowed to use it or touch it. It was too expensive and it wasn't really mine. It was my defencelessness in all of this that hurt.

There was nothing I could do. I remember playing on my own such a lot. When my bike broke there was nobody to fix it, and when it threw me off there was no one to fix me either. I just had to dust myself off, and that very much stayed with me. It was things like that.

Going upstairs every night to my little room, I used to enjoy listening to the humdrum noise of the cars or distant factories, and they were company for me as I went to sleep. I was able to picture a little angel, I think with a child's face, by my bed. She was my comfort because no one came to say goodnight. Then my mum moved into her own little flat, and I remember she said I couldn't stay there because children weren't allowed. And that wasn't heartbreaking, but it was very hard, because of the separation. Then she moved again and took me with her. But the landlord abused her and tried to abuse me, and from then on I somehow never felt properly male.

I was a tearaway before I was 6, and was expelled from my first school. I just remember feeling much rougher than everyone else, and seeing they could read and write and I couldn't. All of these little things were compounding, growing into a knowing that there was stuff missing. I was losing out.

In the changing rooms at primary school I felt I wasn't like other boys. It could have been because this was a white, middle-class area and I was the only coloured kid for miles. The other boys would probably have looked at me because of that. But I just knew it was because of the abusive landlord, and I suppose there may have been other abuse that I've blanked out.

Later I can remember walking past a beautiful church and I could hear the choir singing. I thought, 'I'd so love to sing.' But when I went in and there was the choir and the choirmaster, I thought, 'This is dark,' and also scary. A man and boys – I couldn't. I just had to run, just had to leave. I was already learning people weren't safe, and I didn't feel normal because of those two things.

Also, when my mother came home I would run under the table to avoid whatever it was – poker, belt, hand, umbrella – if I could. That continued until I was about 7. But then one day the social worker came and said he was taking me out for a drive, and he dropped me off at a children's home. And I remember standing in the massive doorway, sobbing. I'd not understood that I wasn't going back to my mother and I was going to be left here, in this big scary place. I don't think something died in me then; I think it was already dead.

You have no control at that age. You do whatever you're told because you're just little and it's all scary and very strange. But after a little while I got used to being there, realizing my mother did not love me. I used to go to sleep crying; I didn't really know why, it just came and it was like, 'I know I must let this cry out.' Apart from that there were no feelings, only the feeling of longing to belong and realizing that I belonged to nobody.

They were good staff in the children's home, but you didn't belong to them. Of course, if they had children, that scuttled it, because you could see them growing up as you grew up, except that they grew up in their family and you grew up in this home without a family.

Eventually the house-parents left, and that threw me completely. They had been quite a strong, consistent help, even though they were just professional and not loving. But they had also abandoned me. I managed to persuade my social worker to move me to where they now were. So I had a history with them that the other kids didn't. But by then I knew that it was all just professional childcare. I knew how to get what I wanted. I had become a professional as well.

Then suddenly I realized that I had no backing, and I was watching older children go out into the adult world and just disappear. I was really scared. I managed to get myself fostered, although it was tough on the family. I was so institutionalized, so impersonal, that I could fake it, but it wasn't real. They could only do real, and on their terms, because they were a close-knit family and had ways of living, so it just lost pace.

I managed to hang on there long enough to move down to the Royal Marines. I knew this was important, because it would make the transition from boy to man and it was another institution, and I could do institution! We had to go to church on Sunday but actually my confession at the end of the day was that there was no God. Life is lived and then you die.

Friends carried me through for a little while, and then I went into care work. It felt like when princes are groomed to be kings. I felt groomed to be a carer and that's what I could do, easily, but life was not really worth it. It was just going through the motions.

Then I met Julie and we got married, had a bit of fun, had some children and struggled financially. We bought a house, which I thought I'd never do. Having a wife and a house, it seemed to me I'd made it. But eventually we decided to separate, because we really weren't doing each other any good. Neither of us could go on any more.

But just before separating, we went to see Peter.

At our first session with Peter, he said that it wasn't his job to keep us together, but he'd help us personally and if we then decided to stay together, so be it. They were golden words, really. That was the first honesty I had heard in a long time, and it did it for me. So I started the journey. He said I had to start by working out what I wanted.

Now I didn't do wanting, didn't know how. I had just bumped into Julie, the house, the kids. As I started to own what I wanted, what I wanted turned into what I didn't have. That was when I discovered all the loss.

I saw that I had no sense of self. I could play the game of living, but not from a 'Mike' point of view. One of the first things Peter shared with me was that I manipulated people to be safe around me and to like me, because if they liked me they wouldn't hurt me. I never found it to be true that they would not hurt me, but I still believed it was the safest way to try and manage people. They still hurt me anyway.

I became aware, doing the *Rapha* journey, that I had set up all these things to try and keep myself safe, but actually inside there was nothing to keep safe. So when people hurt me, it was really strange, because I couldn't work out what they'd hurt. There was no sense of self. Instead there was just a big hole.

I remember deciding that I needed to take one good quality from each of the children's home staff, and copy that in myself. Otherwise, how do you grow up? What do you aspire to? From then on I became bits of other people, and I think that's where the professional carer grooming kicked in. I remember even liking a particular voice on the radio. My accent was different from those around me and I must have modelled it on this radio voice. I quite liked it then and I quite like it now! But even that was false. I had lost me.

Pursuing the *Rapha* journey can show people the 'why' of their present pain, and enable them to recognize the past damage that caused it. It can also show you where you have reinvented yourself in the face of difficulty or danger. You can say sorry, and you can let go of that stuff, and then you can choose to become who the Lord created you to be. To me, that sounded like stepping off a cliff into nothingness, and it took me quite a while to go there, because I thought, 'I've done enough of nothingness.' But eventually I did, because within the community everyone else is in forward motion.

It was here at Christ Church that I had my first sense of hope, ever. And now I see that in other people when they arrive. For the first time there's a hope and a reason for living, and a wanting to *live*, not just survive.

We all have to do homework, using different ways to let go by finding the 'sorry', then giving it to the Lord and asking Him to reveal the reason it is so strong in our lives. In my case, up popped these faces that had betrayed me and hurt me, so I shouted at them and let go of the pain they caused.

You let it go, forgiving those who caused it. You then take time to recover, giving the Lord permission to show you more. I spent many months like that, each time asking the Lord to redeem what had happened, just so that 'I' could come through – who I should have been. And asking the Lord to do that with a strong knowing and sense of hope. This makes it worthwhile asking, because although you're not guaranteed it, in a sense you are. You're beginning to remove the rubbish on the path, so you can let 'you' come through.

I carried a lot of hate towards people (and I work in care!). By the end of my childhood I knew that everybody was dangerous. Which is how it is when you're frightened and abused and have had no adult protection: everybody's a threat, with each situation reinforcing the previous one. You either play them or stay away from them. So nothing weird in that, that's just running the race in an abstract sort of way. None of it fits together and, yeah, you look around and you think, 'How can it not fit together?' I could look at the sky, look at the clouds, the rain, the sun, at the things that grew, and it all fitted together, but none of it fitted for me. I wasn't part of it. So the whole thing called life just made me really angry and bitter and twisted.

One of the stages of my journey was looking at my anger.

I'd just stored it all, managed it, or so I thought. But actually it was poison. A drip of poison hung from everything I said, even when I thought I was being nice. That's because it was in my spirit, in my heart: that everyone's dangerous and abusive, I can't stand them, and worse. Doing the homework has made a huge difference to the way I am around people, and the way they are around me.

Something that I found really hard was realizing that a lot of the bad stuff was what I was choosing. So I've had to say sorry to myself and to others, because in choosing bad for myself I've inevitably chosen bad for others. I have needed to ask the Lord to redeem it, and then I have to deliberately choose good in its place. The Lord wants us 'to dare to dream and to hope for things good'.

I have also had to learn that these bad things do not have to happen to us. They are other people's version of life that they are laying on us. We have a right to good. It's there for the taking, so you can reach out for it. And that's what the Lord intended for you. All the rest was not intended.

Sometimes I have to remind myself that I need to live the life I now can live, and not slip back into the death. By death I mean bad choices, old patterns of thinking. I need to remind myself that I can live at peace with myself and others, without risk or fear of being beaten up or abused spiritually, emotionally, verbally, sexually or physically.

One of the things that my journey has exposed is an immense area of fear. I discovered with Peter's help that all my reactions were based on fear. His approach is to reel off ten or twenty topics in a multiple choice and say, 'Here, try these. Ask the Lord about them, and whichever is hot for you, unpack it.' Then I set to work choosing to believe that it can be different, giving up unrighteous fear.

Sometimes I still find myself slipping back into the

'pleasing them' mode. Then I think, 'Hang on, it doesn't have to be like this. OK, I'm me, I have my thoughts, I have my feelings, I am right and it's OK. I choose to respect myself and I require that other people respect me.'

This takes practice. When I spend time preparing my day with the Lord, I know that I carry an authority in Him, which is me. But if I'm not as well prepared, something will get to me. Then I think, 'OK, Mike, just go away and spend some time with the Lord; come back as me, who I am in the Lord.' People then respond to me completely differently. And it's not as though there are fences put up to keep them off, as in the old days, or flirtation or manipulation of them to be nice'; it's just, 'No, this is how it is. I'm me.'

If I'm going to prepare myself for the day, I need to spend time with the Lord in the morning. I offload my thoughts and then just shut up and ask the Lord to speak to me, because I want to hear Him. I welcome my emotions and their feelings because they are new to me and I want them to stay there. If I haven't been with the Lord for a few days, I have to keep going and spending time with him. It's as if I'm coming back into relationship, and I have to earn that. You don't have to earn anything with the Lord, because it's already there, but for me, that's how it works. I enjoy the Lord, and the authority that I carry in Him, and the effect of that on me and others. When I'm in an exceptionally good place with the Lord I can hear Him all the time, and I just sit chatting to Him. That's a lovely place to be, and it's very fulfilling. Then I know that I've actually maximized who I can be at that time. That's nice, that's good.

My journey till now has been about finding Mike. Now it's mostly about growing Mike. So who is this 'me' that was so painfully absent? How can I describe what 'me' is? It's feelings and it's emotion, a sense of self, of value in myself. I'm worth it. Formerly, it was, 'Well, he's worthless anyway.' Although people might not have verbalized it, that was the feeling. And I found it hard to speak or to have an opinion that was my own. Now my opinion counts, and it gives life.

Some Comments

Christine had lost a part of herself when she was in the womb, but she had been unaware of this loss most of her life. Mike lost himself mainly because of the absence of relationships that should have helped 'call him to himself' in his early life. In both cases it was loss. The issue of loss is by far the greatest in our work. All of us have experienced loss, and most of us do not know how to deal with it. Instead of owning the loss, and admitting this is what has happened, welcoming the feelings and all its pain, we have a tendency to deny how bad it is, push down the pain, then try to get on with life anyway. This 'denial' merely makes the pain worse, and festers in us toxic emotion that may later come back and bite us. Unless we deal with loss correctly, we will be cursed to live out its pain and consequences, while continuing to deny this is the case.

To deal with loss properly we must first admit the loss exists. We call this stage 'owning' the loss. With the intellectual admission that the loss is real, we then need to give our emotion and its feelings permission to surface, with the Lord's help. As the feelings come, they will sometimes flood us, be overwhelming, as though they are too strong to bear. But let them come anyway. You may need to use the empty chair, or begin to write down what you are feeling and thinking. What is key is to own the emotion, giving it to the Lord as you feel it. As we mentioned earlier in the book, what you feel and give to the Lord helps empty the memories of emotion, thereby allowing them to die naturally.

But the healing of loss is not complete until you have recovered the ground that was stolen by the loss. Maybe it means getting a new job, or beginning a new career. Christine, for instance, had to practise saying she had a twin brother; Mike had to find himself and begin to enjoy that person. Healing is complete when we are able to talk about the loss without overwhelming pain, while admitting it really was bad. Owning the loss, and living out its redemption as though it never was, is all part of the redemption.

Notes

[1] We do not advocate 'memory' before birth, or its therapy. But it is evident from the people we have dealt with over the years that many are damaged by such things as violent conception or events in the womb, so they will need to let go emotionally and cathartically of the pain and trauma of these as they perceive them.

[2] We do a great deal of dream interpretation in our work, as it seems to be one of the key ways the Lord has of bringing to the surface unconscious ideas and feelings that we resist owning. The meaning of some dreams is obvious, but others will need interpreting by someone who understands these principles of interpretation.

[3] This is not as strange as it may sound. We all inherit good characteristics from our parents, e.g. looks, interests, abilities, etc. So it should not be a surprise that we also inherit what is bad, such as characteristics in our persona that lead us to certain dark interests, dark gifting or a tendency to see the Enemy as more powerful than the Lord.

Conclusion

The purpose of this book is to introduce you to the idea of a discipleship journey that not only helps you become more like Jesus, but also helps clear some of the baggage that stands between us and God. Once this is removed, as God tells you about it and you act on it, you will also discover that it will help to positively change your relationships with family and friends.

In one sense none of what you have read about in these people's stories is new. There has always been a healing wholeness journey in the church. But many of us do not see the need to change further once we have committed to Christ, even though Scripture and the traditions of the church already have much to teach us about a discipleship that heals through a journey of personal positive change, e.g. Merton's *The Seven Storey Mountain*, Lewis's *Surprised by Joy* and Bunyan's *Pilgrim's Progress*.

Ultimately the teachings of Scripture must be our guide. For instance, the idea of the spiritual house is found in Scripture (Lk. 11:24–26, 2 Tim. 2:20–21, Mt. 7:7–8, Ps. 127:1, Mt. 12:44, Mk. 3:25, Acts 7:49, Heb. 3:6, etc.) and was written about by St Teresa in 1577, under the title of

The Interior Castle. Other ideas, like the value of emotion as God's 'second chance', reflect a Hebrew concept of feelings lost to most of us today. We are currently writing a book on the theme of *Feeling is healing*, based on this Biblical idea. The concept of loss, and our need to redeem it, is a theme found throughout Scripture. Many of the characters of the Old and New Testament suffered loss of various kinds. Also, dream interpretation, which is seen as a spiritual gift, is used in Scripture by people like Daniel.

But other practices in *Rapha* are more contemporary, such as the Gestalt idea of the empty chair, or the concept that we can lose 'ourselves' or be impacted by things that happen to us in the womb. What we have learnt over many years is that such ideas do not seem to be a problem to the Lord, as He uses them frequently in people's lives. The stories, and their outcomes outlined here, are repeated many, many times in CCD and *Rapha*, each with the same experience of the Lord walking and talking, one way or another, with each person who is willing to let Him lead them. It is our experience that God seems to be much more eager to talk to us in any way He can than we are willing to take time to listen to the way He wants to talk to us. So we have learnt to be cautious about trying to specify what we think God should do or use to help make us more like Jesus, or to define what we think is 'Biblical'.

What is most evident on this *Rapha* journey is the place of sin. Its recognition is central to our workshop programmes, and 'sin against oneself' is a Biblical idea that is the experience of all of us on this journey. But we are aware that the idea of sin is not popular today, even in some parts of the church. Here in CCD we often see sin as our unwillingness to change.

What we have done in this book is to ask each of the

people to focus on one issue for their story. This has been difficult for all of them, so you will have noted that in each of the stories, they are frequently referring to other issues they still have to deal with, e.g. Roman and his need to learn to live without his addictions, and Mike needing to know who he really is. Most folk who commit to the journey will need to work through a number of issues, or rooms in their spiritual house. Each issue, though clearly separate, will be connected to others they have already dealt with, or will need to sort in the future. Each person will have between eight and fifteen areas of their life that they will need to clean up. But because we are one whole as people, there is no such thing as discrete sickness. Damage in one area of our life will impact our whole being.

Behind each issue is the importance of spiritual reality. We see two aspects to this: our human spirituality, our human spirit, and the reality of the spiritual world, where God principally dwells. So for us to know Him we must become aware, and willing to begin adopting such thinking. We are first and foremost spiritual beings that have been physically embodied. It is not the other way round. So as spiritual beings we need to own this aspect of our human nature and let the Lord teach us how to awaken our spiritual nature in us. For how can we know a Holy *Spirit* if we do not know spirit in our own lives? The problem many of us face, both in and outside the church, is that we believe darkness is more able to deceive us in such matters than the Lord is able to protect and guide us.

This is one of the reasons why it is so important to walk the road with other people, either in community, discipleship or support groups. We believe that we learn best from people who have already sorted out the issue that we are about to tackle. We call this mentoring (see the *Afterword*). Each of us has much we can learn from one another if we have a teachable spirit and are willing to admit we are in need. In CCD this takes the form of a therapeutic faith community, but you will not need this if you are willing to learn from the workshops, listen to the Lord and allow others to love and support you.

Finally, the journey we and the storytellers in the book are all on is a journey of meeting Jesus, seeking out with His help what is standing in the way of deeper intimacy with Christ. There are many therapeutic journeys we can follow to help us get well, but only one that focuses on Christ as the subject and goal of our journey. What we are saying in this short book is that by allowing Jesus to be at the centre of our life journey, we get to know Him better, while also becoming whole. I can think of no better personal aim in this life than to get to know Christ.

Afterword

Christ Church Deal

The discipleship model that Peter had developed over many years from the late 1960s benefited me (Susan) and is described in my book *Letting God Heal*. That story began with Peter and Mary over fifteen years ago. But in October 1998 the model found a home in Christ Church Deal, when five of us planted this congregation here on the east coast of Kent, UK. All of us were doing the *Rapha* journey, with Peter's help, and wanted to create a safe place for folk like ourselves who were beginning the journey. Almost immediately remarkable things began to happen. From twenty-four adults plus kids, the community doubled in size in the first year and has continued growing ever since, attracting large numbers from Deal, from around the UK and even from overseas. Many of these were poor, emotionally ill, unchurched people, or just tired Christians who had admitted they needed to change.

That in itself was remarkable. But something even more amazing happened. People doing the *Rapha* journey, all being together, created a social dynamic that was more powerful than just the one-to-one support I had had. Many came to CCD with issues similar to mine, but unlike myself found themselves with a church full of people to support them, allowing them to move on at a speed I had not been able to. The social process of the community facilitated faster change in them, as they looked to one another for guidance and support. I had help from Peter, but felt very much alone between sessions. In CCD folk have each other all the time, whenever they need help or support.

This has developed even further over the years, so much so that now we have a large number of 'mentors' in the community, whose specific goal is to help members of the community struggling with issues they have themselves already overcome. This has made CCD a special type of church, with equal numbers of men and women, which the members themselves describe as a *therapeutic faith community*.

For details of our services contact our office at 3 Stanhope Road, Deal, Kent CT14 6AB, UK. Tel: 01304 366512, email: Christchurchdeal@f2s.com or visit our website: www.christchurchdeal.org.

Rapha Workshops and Support Groups

These remarkable events have not been confined to members of our congregation. As we planted CCD we began teaching weekend workshops. The first one was in Peter and Mary's home in Walmer, Kent, quickly followed by other UK locations. But they have now spread to the USA, Europe, and even Turkey. We hold them wherever we are invited to. These are for groups of men or women who want to do the *Rapha* journey. They are designed to be self-empowering, that is, allowing you to do the journey alone, wherever you are. But as in CCD, folk are coming together to support one another, and many of those who have done the introductory workshops are now in support groups.

We offer a range of workshops, alongside the Introductory and 'Toolbox' workshops. These cover a range of subjects, including Womanhood, Meeting Jesus, How to Mentor, and Living with Healing. We have a strong team of folk from CCD and the *Rapha* network able to teach these workshops from personal experience. With over a thousand people already having graduated from these workshops, we will no doubt see these growing even more.

We also offer an extensive range of teaching tapes for those who have completed the workshop, which add extra encouragement to the journey. If you are interested in being on our mailing list, contact our office for a free introductory tape and a list of where and when the workshops are next being held.

Office address: 3 Stanhope Road, Deal, Kent CT14 6AB, UK. Tel 01304 239621. Email Rapha@f2s.com.

Susan B. Williams
Walmer, Kent, UK

BECOMING MORE HUMAN

Exploring the Interface of Spirituality, Discipleship and
Therapeutic Faith Community

PETER R. HOLMES

from emotional

illness to wholeness

letting
GOD HEAL

Susan B Williams
Peter R Holmes